Fathomsuns

Fadensonnen a

PAUL CELAN

Fathomsuns
Fadensonnen
and
Benighted
Eingedunkelt

Translated by Ian Fairley

CARCANET

This edition published in Great Britain in 2001 by
Carcanet Press Limited
4th Floor, Conavon Court
12–16 Blackfriars Street
Manchester M3 5BQ

A CIP catalogue record for this book
is available from the British Library

ISBN 1 85754 504 4

The publisher acknowledges financial assistance
from the Arts Council of England

Set in Palatino by XL Publishing Services, Tiverton
Printed and bound in England by SRP Ltd, Exeter

Contents

Contents

Contents

EINGEDUNKELT   BENIGHTED

VIER GEDICHTE AUS DEM UMKREIS VON EINGEDUNKELT   FOUR POEMS FROM THE PENUMBRA OF BENIGHTED

Paul Celan

Celan was born Paul Antschel in Czernowitz, former capital of the autonomous Habsburg province of Bukovina, on 23 November 1920. His family belonged to a Jewish community which had grown in strength and number over nearly 150 years of Austrian rule. The Paris Peace Conference of 1919 assigned the region to Romania. In 1940, as a result of the Hitler–Stalin pact, Czernowitz was occupied by Soviet troops, and in the following year, with the collapse of the pact, by German and Romanian forces. In 1944 northern Bukovina, including Czernowitz, was annexed by the Soviet army to the Ukraine, of which it remains part.

Having visited France as a medical student in 1938, Celan returned to Czernowitz in the summer of 1939, taking up the study of Romance languages and literatures after the outbreak of war. The Antschel family lived in the city until 1942, when both parents were deported to a concentration camp in the Transnistria region of the Ukraine. Celan's father died of typhus; his mother was shot when no longer able to work. Their son was conscripted into a series of Romanian labour camps between 1942 and 1944.

After the war Celan emigrated to Bucharest, where he worked as a translator from Russian into Romanian, and in his poems first adopted the anagram of his Romanian surname, Ancel. Celan escaped from Bucharest to Vienna in December 1947, and in 1948 issued his first collection of verse, *Der Sand aus den Urnen*, which he immediately withdrew because of printing errors. In the same year he settled in Paris, where he later taught German literature at the École Normale Supérieure. He married the graphic artist Gisèle de Lestrange in 1952. In 1958 Celan was awarded the Bremen Literature Prize, and in 1960 the Georg Büchner Prize, Germany's highest literary award; the speeches made on each occasion constitute Celan's principal statements on his poetry. In April 1970 Paul Celan committed suicide by drowning in the Seine.

Celan published seven major volumes of verse: *Mohn und Gedächtnis* (1952), *Von Schwelle zu Schwelle* (1955); *Sprachgitter* (1959), *Die Niemandsrose* (1963), *Atemwende* (1967), *Fadensonnen*

(1968), and *Lichtzwang* (1970). Since his death the Celan Estate has issued or reissued his earliest and last poetry, prose writings, verse translations, and several volumes of correspondence. A critical edition of his work is in the process of publication.

Acknowledgements

This translation was made possible through the kindness and good counsel of Raymond Hargreaves, to whom I offer it as a gift of thanks. My wife Jenny listened unconditionally. Don Burbidge taught me how to read. And Michael Schmidt gave his vital moral support.

In a number of translations I have learned from, and am most grateful to, the example of Michael Hamburger and John Felstiner.

Paul Celan

Fathomsuns

Fadensonnen

When and Where?
Paul Celan's *Fadensonnen*

Every question must ask itself after the where and when.

Paul Celan

Fadensonnen, published in 1968, was Paul Celan's sixth and most extensive collection of verse, presenting 105 poems arranged in five constituent cycles. These poems, written between September 1965 and June 1967, and offered in order of their composition, comprise the last major sequence released in the poet's lifetime. They follow *Atemwende* [*Breathturn*], issued in 1967, and are followed by *Lichtzwang* [*Lightforce*], which had been proposed for publication before Celan's suicide in April 1970. All three works practise the aggravated controversions of sense and syntax which characterise his late style, suggesting a poetry which has turned against its own lyric powers. To date, however, *Fadensonnen* is the least well represented in the realms of both critical commentary and translation into English.

One index of the volume's relative immunity to address is provided by its notice in the *Times Literary Supplement* of 27 February 1969. Here, the anonymous reviewer likens Celan's verse to Provençal *trobar clus* – an elaborately 'closed' or riddling form of poetic invention – and continues, in the same mode of respectful unease: 'Celan has consistently won new shades of meaning from the German language, has made it perform in previously unheard and even unsuspected ways; but this magical German of his does tend to be an esoteric *Geheimsprache* whose associations are known to the poet alone.' I should like to take my bearings from this review's difficulty with Celan, for it points to difficulties in the poems which, as Michael Hamburger observes, 'are part of what they say and do'.[1] To describe Celan's poetry as a *Geheimsprache* – a private, secret, or magical language – is to recognise that such writing is not easy to locate; for the place from which it speaks – the home, or *Heim*, of poetry, however fragile that may be – is secreted within the privacy of the *Geheim*. Location is held, if not withheld, in parenthesis. Celan's best-known remark on his poetry cautions that it is 'ganz und gar nicht hermetisch' – 'absolutely not hermetic' – a protest against its critical misconstruction which he was later to repeat in the case of *Fadensonnen*.[2] But Celan also confessed that he found it hard to 'let go' of the latter work.[3] Its unsurrendering qualities ensure that the question of how we are to place *Fadensonnen* remains at issue. In quest of an answer, however, it is first necessary to ask where, upon entering this poetry, we are taken.

These questions are implicit in the much debated poem, written in 1963 and first published in 1965, which bequeaths *Fadensonnen* its title:

FADENSONNEN	THREAD-SUNS
über der grauschwarzen Ödnis.	over the gray-black wasteland.
Ein baum-hoher Gedanke	A tree-high thought
greift sich den Lichtton: es sind	strikes the note of light: there are
noch Lieder zu singen jenseits der Menschen.	still songs to sing beyond mankind.[4]

If readings of this poem share any common ground, it is by way of reponse to the principal question which the writing puts: where are we to place (or understand) the threshold beyond which we are 'beyond / mankind'? Grammatically, the poem describes a terrain of possibility. The formula 'es sind / [...] zu singen' describes songs which either can, ought or must be sung, each sense bearing differently on the temporal location and tendency of the poem's 'tree- / high thought', which may be taken as indicative of a present or directed imperatively toward a future. 'Noch' likewise sounds with the chromatics of consolation, expectancy, impatience and endurance. Are there still, as there once were, songs to be sung? Or are these songs as yet unsung; is their time still to come?

More accurately, the poem puts no questions to us, but rather asks questions of us. How are we to take it? Again, *how* implies a certain *where*. The 'gray-black wasteland' and the 'thread-suns' above it may be located on this side or on that side ('jenseits') of the human threshold. It may be that we are already beyond the 'beyond', in that 'Unland' of spindle-trees described in Celan's HAWDALAH.[5] The place of the poem's 'tree- / high thought' is, then, *utopian*, in a sense literally meant, for it can only be established in relation to an uncertain negation; it is a thought which, possibly, has nowhere to go save 'beyond'. Not only does this thought dislocate the horizon of our expectation – who on earth is to sing these songs 'beyond / mankind'? – but, in its very conception, it appears to locate itself between two worlds, at home in neither. The poem's lexis is itself an index of this condition. As Judith Ryan has claimed, the word 'Fadensonnen' does not represent an object given or received in the world of nature.[6] 'Lichtton' is likewise a compound of apparently unlike things. Light is not usually heard, nor sound seen, unless in the beyond of metaphor, as, perhaps, is the 'light in sound' and 'sound-like power in light' of Coleridge's 'The Eolian Harp'. Recently, however, Pierre Joris has drawn attention to the technical status of 'Lichtton' within cinematography, where it refers to 'sound on film', the encoding of sound in terms of light values.[7] The poem has the capacity to accommodate strangeness on the near side of metaphor. Yet to one side again of this embodiment of 'Lichtton', what startles in such terms is that, in the language of phenomenology, they 'intend', and so come to constitute, the thing they describe.

Despite Ryan's claim that 'Fadensonnen' 'exists solely as a word, not as an object', it evidently proposes a world which is the case within the poem's sphere of apprehension. Asking to be held together with 'Fadensonnen', as part of the same sphere, are the non-compound and this-worldly plurals 'Lieder' and 'Menschen'. It is important to understand that the last term signifies *people* before the more abstract, collectively singular 'mankind' of the translation given above. 'Menschen' is a word which resists the conceptual containment of 'mankind' while nonetheless engaging its values. For humanity is here in dispute: 'Menschen' resonates with the Yiddish (and indeed Enlightenment) sense of *Mensch* – good person – but also with the National Socialist perversion of *menschlich*, a category exclusive of, among others, Jews. As a collective plural, 'Menschen' is a term upon which we cannot set limits, unsettling any bid to house or legislate for humanity in the bad infinity of 'mankind'. The poem may seem to occupy the impossible ground of paradox, but it also discovers the grounds which make paradox apparent: we are in a place beyond humanity which, in so far as it can be (poetically) imagined or acknowledged, humanity may also have created.

Just what is beyond mankind? If the poem's utopian voice can be differently inflected, that is in part because different voices may be heard within it. The most unmistakable and immediately affirmative of these is Rilke's. The first of the *Sonette an Orpheus* begins:

Da stieg ein Baum. O reine Übersteigung!
O Orpheus singt! O hoher Baum im Ohr!
Und alles schwieg. Doch selbst in der Verschweigung
ging neuer Anfang, Wink und Wandlung vor.

[*A tree rose there. O pure surmounting!* / *O Orpheus sings! O high tree in the ear!* / *And all was silent. But from that silence* / *came new beginning, beckoning and change.*] Celan's 'baum- / hoher' echoes Rilke's 'hoher Baum'. The solar threads of 'Fadensonnen' become, in an Orphic context, instrumental to lyric; they are strings of light to be plucked and sounded. To my ear, this lyric inference invokes in turn the psalms of exile, and asks that Celan's poem be read in response to Psalm 137: 'We hanged our harps upon the willows [...]. For there they that carried us away captive required of us a song.' It can be argued, however, that the poem is unwilling to make a home of any of these contexts; any place located or projected 'beyond / mankind' is equally beyond exile or any populated Hades. Erich Fried's lyric retort to Celan protests this seeming negation: 'Lieder / gewiß / auch jenseits / unseres Sterbens [...] // Doch nicht ein einziges Lied / jenseits der Menschen' [*Songs* / *yes* / *even beyond* / *our death* [...] // *But not one song* / *beyond mankind*].[8] Fried recognises that Celan at once invokes and confounds the Orphic propitiation of death. But propitiation is less in question if one reads 'Menschen' with the sarcasm which it allows; and death is perhaps better proposed as an unspoken condition of the poem rather than its subject. The relationship of FADENSONNEN to its predecessor poem is hence a matter of continuity and chiasmus, just as Rilke's 'hoher Baum' is inverted as a thought which appears (impossibly) to refine upon his own 'reine Übersteigung'.

Affirmation and negation are not easily disintricated here or elsewhere in Celan's work. Yet we are returned, by the critical detour its very strangeness has provoked, to the continuity which, in the plainest of terms – 'noch' – FADENSONNEN affirms: 'there are / *still* songs to sing beyond / mankind'. This statement may itself recall the epigram to the second part of Brecht's *Svendborger Gedichte* (1939): 'In den finsteren Zeiten / Wird da auch gesungen werden? / Da wird auch gesungen werden. / Von den finsteren Zeiten' [*In dark times* / *Will there still be songs?* / *There will still be songs.* / *Of dark times*].[9] Brecht's epigram precedes 'Deutsches Lied' with its disabused opening line, 'Sie sprechen wieder von großen Zeiten', words whose critical distance measures the poet's exile from Germany. For Brecht, affirmation is made in, but not of, negation; renewal is regarded darkly, and its prospect must remain on the far side of present horizons. If we are, in FADENSONNEN, already beyond humanity (as, potentially, we always are), there is no immediate getting beyond this condition. The transformational power of the Orphic lyric, its command over the natural world, is not foremost in Celan's invocation of Rilke; where, in Rilke, song calls forth silence – and from that, 'new beginning' – from the beasts of the forest, Celan's poem describes a charred 'wasteland', an unregenerate no man's land presenting no life to be summoned. The dominion of song is divorced from and located *on this side* of any human dominion over nature.

In one account of his project, Celan maintains that his language 'doesn't transfigure [*verklärt nicht*], doesn't "poeticise", it names and places, it attempts to measure the range of the given and the possible'. But far from renouncing the power of words to work on the world, Celan is intent on a particular task: 'Reality doesn't exist [*Wirklichkeit ist nicht*], it must be sought and attained'.[10] Language maps the 'contour' of possibility within the domain of the real – an attention to actuality which has much to do with testing and establishing limits. The poem is, for Celan, a means of 'orientation' in and through the world; he plots his course dialogically, navigating by way of address to what lies before and beyond him. To establish the *sense* of this poetry, located on the threshold of language and being, is thus to determine its sense of *direction*, in time as well as space, toward the subject of its address. In his 'Bremen Speech' of 1958, Celan observes of his writing: 'Whenever I ask myself the sense [*Sinn*] of it, I remind myself that this implies the question as to which sense is clockwise' [*die Frage nach dem Uhrzeigersinn*]. The question of clockwise bears upon the here and now of the poem, its point of arrival or departure, for 'poems are *en route* [*unterwegs*]: they are headed toward'.[11] In *Fadensonnen* that point is also one of interrogation. Several poems observe the uncertain measure of time in images of stasis or entropy, and even where, as in DIE RAUCHSCHWALBE (p. 224), time moves forward, marking a significant hour of release, it does so in defiance of conventional mechanics: 'the One of the sky-clock / flew to the hour-hand, / deep into the chime'. With clockwise in question, poetic inquiry makes, in Celan's words, toward 'something open, inhabitable, an approachable you [*ein ansprech-bares Du*], perhaps, an approachable reality'. Direction is sought or found in relation to this second-person reality, always engaged in the familiar form, either singular *du* or plural *ihr*.

More than half the poems in *Fadensonnen* name or presuppose a second person. The space and time of lyric apostrophe are themselves engaged in this address, and nowhere more imperatively than in the collection's opening poem:

AUGENBLICKE, wessen Winke,	INSTANTS whose eyewink
keine Helle schläft.	no brightness sleeps.
Unentworden, allerorten,	Increate, in every place,
sammle dich,	gather yourself,
steh.	stay. (p. 30)

The first line of AUGENBLICKE proposes an immediate disorientation, against the grain of its own apodictic voice. If that voice arrests attention, allowing little space for response save enactment, the conditions which prompt it remain grammatically and syntactically unfixed. This is a poem which has to do with the uncertain nature of signs. In the phrase 'wessen Winke' – 'whose signals' – the pronoun (relative or interrogative) normally predicts either a question – whose? – or a clause. But the expected question never arrives. There follows a properly discontinuous and intransitive statement of the case: 'no brightness sleeps'. 'Wessen' thereby inaugurates a never-completed clause whose status remains unresolved. Are these 'Winke' the subject of a foreshortened question, asked of or directed to 'Augenblicke'; or are they subordinate to 'Augenblicke', which is taken to govern the sentence as an apostrophised or merely observed subject?

The poem establishes a sound world more securely than any world of sense. Its metrical symmetries, grounded in the repeated patterns of the first and third lines, anchor a network of half-rhymes which, against their own obscurity of location, assert affinity in contiguity. As 'Augenblicke' and 'Winke' are, quizzically, cast together, their relationship must necessarily remain conjectural; conjecture likewise governs the movement between lines one and two (and beyond). Yet incantation makes actual the unmediated and elliptical nature of these connections. This drive to actuality informs the poem's literalising tendency. Its instants, or 'Augenblicke', describe the duration of the eye's vigil, the time it takes the eye to light on and to light a scene – an action as instinctual and involuntary as blinking. Recalling (as does blink) a root sense of shining or gleaming, 'Blicke' anticipates the 'brightness' of line two. (A later poem, UMWEG- / KARTEN (p. 44), ends with the echoic and cognate 'Ein rechtes Auge / blitzt' – 'A right eye / flashes', with lightning). This first line also projects a semantic parallel between 'Blicke' and 'Winke', even if the home of these latter signals remains grammatically in question. Taken together, however, lines one and two have the quality of something unseeing or unseen, blinded or blinding, as if something or someone were in view but unperceived – such as the subject or possible object of this period.

To suppose that the obscure subject of 'Winke' is a godly eye, itself out of sight, would be to speculate in the dark. But in an unintelligible world, amid signs of uncertain notice, that is the only kind of speculation authenticated by Celan's poetry. We have, as one point of reference, Hölderlin's 'Rousseau': 'Winke sind / Von Alters her die Sprache der Götter' [*signs have / ever been the language of the gods*]. Hölderlin's presence in Celan's writing has been much remarked on, and instances of *Augenblick*, *Augenlicht* and *Augenwink* in the earlier poet all bear suggestively on the present poem. But our surmise is arguably more visible in draft, where one version has 'AUGENBLICKE, Istigkeiten, / keine Rose schläft.'[12] The image of the rose in Celan's verse implicates not only a German Romantic but also a specifically Jewish tradition. In the latter context the rose may be received as an emblem of the *Shekhinah*, the immanent presence of God (from the Hebrew *shakhan*, to dwell or rest) which accompanies Israel into exile. In Franz Rosenzweig's modern paraphrase, the *Shekhinah* involves the separation or alienation of God from himself: 'he gives himself away to his people, he shares in their sufferings, sets forth with them into the agony of exile'.[13] This wandering presence is most often apprehended in its shining, 'sparks of the original divine light being scattered about the world'. 'Istigkeiten', which might be glossed as 'essences' – instances of ontological presence, realisation or reality – adumbrates a similar possibility in 'Winke', the term on which Celan settled in preference. Grimm records *Istigkeit* as a nineteenth-century revival of the Middle German *Istikeit*; and Lexer's *Mittelhochdeutsches Handwörterbuch* cites Meister Eckhart as the sole authority for both this term and its adjective *istic/istig*. Adding further point to the theological tenor of Celan's quarrying is the anagrammatic closeness of *istig* and *itzig*, an archaic synonym for *jetzig* – meaning 'of the moment' – whose sense in Yiddish extends to 'one and the same'. The homonym *Itzig* is, moreover, a derogatory word for 'Jew' derived from the forename *Isaak*.

It remains, of course, to acknowledge that this semantic constellation is much less present in the poem's final version. We read in Celan's poetry what it shows us; it is legible – intelligible

– in the same measure that it is taken as literally intended. The difficulty of this literalism is not the secreting of context behind text, but rather the letter's aspiration beyond its own immediate condition, a drive which measures the literal – real – boundaries of that condition. As we have already noted, Celan claimed that his work was in no way hermetic; in refusing an occult poetic, the poet is released to address an occulted world. The poem's spell is cast to dispel. Celan's incantatory, summoning voice engages one world in the name of another.

AUGENBLICKE summons a 'you' to readiness and possible resistance, the imperative 'steh' signalling most immediately 'stand', but also, among other possibilities, 'remain (still)' and 'come or bring to a standstill'. The here and now of apostrophe addresses, and perhaps aims to redress, several senses of this person's presence in time and space. 'You' (the 'brightness' of line two?) is in every place, but is also all over the place, not simply omnipresent but dispersed as if in panic. (Indeed the frequency of *du* in Celan's verse may speak of, as well as to, a certain panic.) 'You' implies an 'I' speaking either to some other or to the self as another. Here AUGENBLICKE, which at one point was included in the draft of *Atemwende*, is in dialogue with EINMAL, the last poem in that preceding collection:

EINMAL,	ONCE
da hörte ich ihn,	I heard him,
da wusch er die Welt,	he was washing the world,
ungesehn, nachtlang,	unseen, nightlong,
wirklich.	real.
Eins und Unendlich,	One and Infinite,
vernichtet,	annihilated,
ichten.	ied.
Licht war. Rettung	Light was. Salvation.[14]

EINMAL describes a moment of salvation in the first person but in the past tense. According to Celan (as related by Michael Hamburger), this first person is, in the penultimate line, itself found in the past imperfect, as the third person plural of the verb 'to (declare) I' – its subject being the annihilated pair of 'One and Infinite'. Grimm's *Wörterbuch* cites *ichen* in that sense, but also gives a single example of *ichten* as, in effect, the infinitive antonym of *vernichten* ('to annihilate'), a linguistic turn which approximates to mystical speculation on creation *ex nihilo*. In this reading, just as the One is annihilated, so annihilation and salvation are at one – a paradox realised in the movement from 'vernichtet' to 'Licht' through a verb (now taken as a third person plural in the *present* tense) which exposes the common term in each: 'ich(t)'. At the same time, the verbal operation of an 'I' – hence the speaker's very testimony – repeats the annihilation of a transcendent 'One and Infinite' into multiple 'I's. By confounding time in its possible senses, 'ichten' opens a singular moment of salvation to more than one reading, summoning this past event into the present as a question yet to be answered. If 'once' – the one instant of EINMAL – looks, as it must, to an 'again', this is already to establish the uniqueness of every one act of witness or experience, to determine on the non-identity of these moments (*as* terms) even in their conjunction: 'Once again / Do I behold these steep and lofty cliffs'.

The drive to instantiate poetic utterance within its own moment – time or place – is surely a generative principle in Celan's sequence-building. This mode is all the more explicit when *Fadensonnen* is revealed as, with some overlapping, a chronological series. AUGENBLICKE announces the volume as a sequence of moments in eclipse – such, at least, is one reading of 'no brightness sleeps' – which nonetheless look to, and occasionally record, the experience of illumination. The imperative 'gather yourself' urges a condition in which *you* might realise itself as *I*, thereby enacting the illumination which, waiting to be realised as literal, is potential within every instant. The temporal status of this second person is described by 'unentworden', a term which raises contradiction to the second power and possibly beyond. The principal senses of the now archaic root verb *entwerden* are 'to escape, vanish or perish'. In each case, the prefix *ent-*, which indicates movement out of one state and into another, carries a negative charge. This movement has to do with becoming, or *werden*, a verb which here achieves the status of an ontological category: becoming escapes, or is escaped, or both. But however we construe it, the operation is itself negated within Celan's compound 'unent-'. Several readings of this double negative are available. Most plainly conceived, it describes a 'you' for whom the state of escape or absence – even that of death – has been cancelled. More difficult to grasp is the relation of becoming to ending proposed by the phonetic equivalence, in context, of *ent-* and *end-*, and its cancellation in turn. 'You' may have become without end, or may have become an end no more. In either case, 'you' has become the term of ending.

'Unentworden', in this reading, discloses the person of God 'in every place'. A 'you' in every sense dark is suddenly lit; a benighted world is illumined. Something of this possibility – of the double moment, each potential in the other, which the poem appears to contain – is evident in Grimm's entry for *entwerden*, and not least in those passages cited from Meister Eckhart. The most substantive of these is from Eckhart's tractate on the story of the loaves and fishes, which he allegorises as the five duties of the Christian and the two powers of the soul. Through its under-standing and will, the soul has the power both to comprehend God and to become one with Him 'above knowledge'. From this state Adam fell: 'But now all creatures which came forth from God must strive with all their powers to make one man who shall return into the union wherein Adam was.' Restitution is figured as a gathering in Christ; through Christ, all men may be one man, and that man God. It is in considering God's this-worldly emana-tion in the persons of the Trinity that Eckhart elaborates upon the paradoxical relationship between divine being and becoming:

> God is from himself eternally and the Father made all things from nothing. That he is in himself he is by his own nature, which is free from becoming and becomes not any thing [*allen dingen entwirt*], and all things' becoming ends in not-becoming [*aller dinge werden endet an dem entwerdenne*]. The Son is the same as the Father except that he receives from the Father all that he has and of all becoming he is the form. Withal he is one in the not-becoming. The Holy Ghost is the tie between the Father and the Son and is one with them in the not-becoming; he is the author and agent of becoming in eternity and time. This temporal becoming ends in eternal not-becoming [*zîtlîche werden endet an dem êwigen entwer-denne*], and the eternal not-becoming is the work of the eternal nature and has neither end nor beginning.[15]

Eckhart strenuously exploits the contradictions of *entwerden*, finding in 'entwirt' both 'issues from' and 'becomes (not)'. At the nexus of two contiguous orders, temporal and eternal, the verb takes on a necessarily paradoxical status. Whereas in this passage 'temporal becoming ends in eternal not-becoming', in another tractate Eckhart locates *entwerden* on the negative path to becoming with God: 'Where God finds His will He gives Himself to him and passes into him with all that is His. And the more we grow out of our own [*des unsern entwerden*], the more truly we grow [*werden*] in this.'[16] Celan's 'unentworden' inhabits a no less vertiginous realm of possibility, and may describe emanation, extinction or the as yet unrealised condition of either. While 'unent-' is most economically translated through the latinate *inex-*, it is only when the parts of this compound are fully set at odds, and *in* comes to express dwelling as well as cancellation, that its full range is realised. My own 'increate' is, in its recollection of Milton's 'Bright essence of bright effluence increate', closer to Eckhart's 'entwerdenne' until we concede to its prefix the sense of transacted negation – out of one state, into another – at which point we approach the potentially reflexive double negative of 'unentworden'. Some such operation is, for Eckhart, central to the apprehension of God: 'To define the nature of something created is at the same time to say what it is not, while in defining the nature of God, the uncreated, we negate the principle of negation itself.'[17] Eckhart follows Thomas Aquinas in distinguishing between an undifferentiated Godhead, who does not create, and the Three Persons in whose form he appears as creator. Hence a statement such as 'Gott wirt und entwirt' may be glossed in terms of the disappearance of a triune God, so that only the One, or a co-terminous Nothing ('nihtes niht'), remains.[18] Unity with God is celebrated as *innewonen* – we dwell in God and he in us – a condition which is conceivably the end of *entwerden*, and thereby 'unentworden'. If seeming contraries here bear analogical relation to one another, this is because, for Eckhart, analogy is intrinsic to the relation of God to his creatures, as all things emanate from the One in which they continue to participate. The attribute of oneness does not affirm anything of God, for that would supplement the One to which nothing can be added. Analogy thus participates in the paradoxical inadequacy of any (affirmative) naming of or approach to God in this world. Conceived as 'daz ungewortet Wort', God's best likeness becomes the image of his 'uncreated' ('ungeschaffen' or 'ungemachet') birth in the soul, akin to the kindling of a divine spark within us.[19]

The possibilities surmised in Celan's 'unentworden' themselves perform a relay between the created and the uncreated, however understood, not least because the poem's 'you' may be either creaturely or divine. But Eckhart's eschatology is not Celan's; the poem's invocation of both Jewish and Christian mysticism troubles the stream of their sometime confluence, and the sum of readings proposed for 'unentworden' is compounded by referential uncertainty as to any *beyond* or *before* which that preterite form, if it is such, might suppose – other than, of course, the event of preterition. The resolute immanence of the poem's unframed moment, its address to, or apprehension of, a plurality of 'moments', accounts for why AUGENBLICKE may appear so descriptively groundless while evidently fixing upon what is present to it. The pursuit of analogy which is urged by, and endeavours to constellate, the poem's grammatically discontinuous symmetries, is returned to a residual literalism which, in the first place, grounds this speculation. Celan gives us what is, or remains, the case, echoing his statement in 'The Meridian' that the poem 'holds its ground on its own margin', pulling back 'from an "already-no-more" [*Schon-nicht-mehr*] into a "still-here"' [*Immernoch*].[20]

Our attempt to locate AUGENBLICKE in terms of these coordinates is borne out by the gloss on its title-word offered by several place poems in *Fadensonnen*. Hendaye, a town on the Atlantic border of France and Spain, is the occasion of the following appeal:

HENDAYE

Die orangene Kresse,
steck sie dir hinter die Stirn,
schweig den Dorn heraus aus
   dem Draht,
mit dem sie schöntut, auch
   jetzt,
hör ihm zu,
eine Ungeduld lang.

HENDAYE

The orange cress
plant behind your brow,
quiet the barb from the wire
which adorns it, even now,
and this attend,
impatience long.

(p. 52)

The poem's final line, 'eine Ungeduld lang', is a variation on the everyday formula *einen Augenblick lang*, 'for an instant'. The barb silenced from the wire must be listened to for the period of 'impatience'. In a prior dislocation of the expected word or phrase, this barb is, more accurately, a thorn. The conjunction of 'Dorn' and 'Draht' is also found in the volume's last poem, DENK DIR, where an internee 'commits homeland to heart [...] / against / every barb in the wire'. In each work, an image of barbed wire (*Stacheldraht*), whether fencing a border or a concentration camp, is given an emblematic charge which brings to mind Christ's crown of thorns and, within Celan's canon, the thorn over which, in PSALM, the 'no one's rose', with its 'heaven-ravaged' stamen ('Staubfaden'), has sung.[21] In counselling impatience or resistance, HENDAYE makes an association between sacrifice and confinement which implies that sacrifice (or its ideology) is itself held to imprison. The poem's focus becomes the limit of endurance, a limit looked to but not yet passed beyond. Though not necessarily imminent, this end is possibly immanent within impatience, which articulates a present want where patience (that popular mark of the saint) might suffer its continued unfulfilment. On the other hand, impatience, the more finite and perhaps worldly quality, does not always end in its want being met. Bearing on the poem from a properly non-temporal perspective, 2 Peter cautions, in the Geneva translation: 'The Lord is not slack concerning his promise, [...] but is patient toward us, and [...] would all men come to repentance' (3,9). In the King James Bible 'patient' is changed to 'long-suffering'. HENDAYE may have little time for either version.

The juxtaposition of two quite different temporal measures – an impatience and an instant – induces a form of interpretive vertigo when, abruptly, each looms sheer on the horizon of the other. Vertigo, that momentary confusion of far and near, performs a revolution on the horizon of the known. Distances are questioned and limits displaced. Celan is recorded as saying that 'The poem is voiceless and voiced at the same time. It is between the two. It must yet become voice.'[22] It becomes more of a voice, I suggest, when we articulate the voiceless in the voiced, 'Augenblick' in 'Ungeduld', 'Itzigkeit' in 'Istigkeit', and so on. On another occasion, when asked to respond to Hans Magnus Enzensberger's claim that Germany's political system was beyond mere reform, Celan stated the first conditions of change in terms that also serve to describe his poetry: 'In Germany, it begins here and now [*hier und heute*], with the individual.'[23] This triangulation determines the coordinates of poetic utterance as much as any other social practice; the language of poetry 'names and places [*nennt und setzt*], it attempts to measure the range of the given and the possible'. In the here and now, space is measured by time and time by space. Singular terms, claiming exclusive dominion over a particular moment, are brought into relation.

The nexus of one such moment is described in the second of two poems situated in Pau:

PAU, SPÄTER   PAU, LATER

In deinen Augen-   In the corners of your
winkeln, Fremde,   eye, outland,
der Albigenserschatten –   the Albigensian shadow –

nach	to
dem Waterloo-Plein,	the Waterloo-Plein,
zum verwaisten	to the orphaned
Bastschuh, zum	espadrille, to the
mitverhökerten Amen,	Amen thrown in,
in die ewige	I sing you
Hauslücke sing ich	through the eternal gap
dich hin:	between houses:
daß Baruch, der niemals	that Baruch, he who never
Weinende	weeps,
rund um dich die	may grind to right the
kantige,	square-edged,
unverstandene, sehende	scopic, uncomprehended
Träne zurecht-	tear around
schleife.	you. (p. 56)

'In deinen Augen- / winkeln, Fremde, / der Albigenserschatten':
these first lines reconfigure 'AUGENBLICKE, wessen Winke' as
disquietingly plural corners of an eye haunted by shadows of the
past. The 'Albigensian shadow' is cast, in two further paragraphs,
on the Amsterdam of Baruch Spinoza and on the Nazi expulsion
of Amsterdam's Jews. In a process replayed in reverse, so that last
things are met with first ('nach' suggests 'coming after' as well as
'moving toward'), the poem translates from Pau to the Waterloo-
Plein, a square which gives its name to the flea-market in
Amsterdam's Jewish quarter close to the Murrano synagogue
from which Spinoza was himself expelled. The 'you' of the first
paragraph is sung through, or into, the 'eternal gaps' between
houses whose demolition speaks of a history implicated in the
second paragraph; on visiting Amsterdam in May 1964 Celan
discovered at Spinoza's birthplace only an empty lot.[24] 'Fremde'
can mean both 'strange or foreign place' and 'strange woman';
however we read it, the foreign is apostrophised in familiar terms,
implying a synapsis between addressee and speaker which is
compounded by 'sing ich / dich hin'. Association conceives the
poem's 'you' as itself a compound of here and there, now and
then. For, directed toward both an 'orphaned / espadrille' and
the 'Amen' which, 'thrown in', seals its exchange, this 'you'
accompanies these things in more than their mere abandonment
to one another. The poem is faithful to those Jewish Codes of Law
which stipulate that 'Amen' must not be 'orphaned' from the
blessing or benediction to which it is spoken in response.[25]

Fathomsuns / Fadensonnen

In its final paragraph, the poem's work of housing and of mourning converges. 'You' is sung into the 'ewige / Hauslücke' – absences which may house in the absence of any house – so that Baruch (Spinoza) may grind around this second person a 'scopic / tear'. Marlies Janz has observed the interlingual pun potential in this place-name doubly full (*plein*) of water / *l'eau*.[26] Overspill is metonymically taken up in the tear which, if once housed in the corner of the eye, cannot now be contained. It is, however, for Baruch (Benedictus: 'the blessed one'), identified here as 'he who never / weeps', to ensure that this tear will contain and focus the grief which prompts it. Spinoza 'grinds aright' a tear which otherwise might blur the vision. By that token the poem invites us to imagine its own vision as Spinozan, a philosophy for which 'immanence is only immanent to itself', which 'neither surrenders to the transcendent nor restores it, inspires the fewest illusions […] and erroneous perceptions'.[27] Mourning dwells in a lens-like tear with, we may infer, an optical compass of 360 degrees.

PAU, SPÄTER discovers a beyond in the present of its address to a strange person or place. It throws into question our understanding of 'place poem', projecting the poem beyond its avowed location even as it discovers the latter as the ground of the former. In effect, this ectopic operation enfolds the elsewhereness of Pau in the poem's here and now, describing a line of topological relation which situates both it and the Waterloo-Plein on a common circumference, neither this nor that side of beyond. Another determinedly local association, preposterous in the very logic of its metonymy, is pursued in the preceding poem:

PAU, NACHTS

Die Unsterblichkeitsziffer, von
   Heinrich
dem Vierten in
den Schildkrötenadel gewiegt,
höhnt eleatisch
hinter sich her.

PAU, NIGHT

The cipher of immortality,
   cradled in
the tortoise athel by Henry
the Fourth,
trails Eleatic insults
in its wake.   (p. 54)

The castle at Pau preserves, in a room said to have been the birthchamber of Henry the Fourth, the infant Henry's tortoise-shell cradle. Celan's poem sardonically likens the 'cipher [number] of immortality' which Henry rocks in the 'tortoise athel' to Zeno's tortoise – now elevated to nobility – trailing 'Eleatic insults / in its wake'. Immortality is, it seems, always one step ahead of us. But the poem effectively returns the cipher's sarcasm, recognising a mortality (*Sterblichkeit*), and thereby a process, which Eleatic paradox would otherwise deny. Zeno argued for the 'One', and against plurality and motion, by confounding two distinct conceptions of infinity and so collapsing time and space. The conundrum is familiar: if a tortoise has the start of Achilles, it can never be caught, for by the time Achilles has run the distance advanced by the tortoise, the tortoise will always have advanced further. Hence Achilles may run *ad infinitum* without ever overtaking the tortoise. Zeno's premise is based upon the infinite subdivision of finite distance, whereas his conclusion assumes an absolute infinity of distance. In PAU, NACHTS the cipher of immortality, a number with no end, is deciphered through its ludicrous approximation to historical contingency. By virtue of the idiosyncrasy of its detail, the poem is counter-hermetic in intent; it performs a negation of the negation which is 'Unsterblichkeit'. Here we can distinguish between the dialectical intent of Celan's poetry, directed against the all-embracing singularity of the 'One', and that of the eschatologies which his work engages and from which it draws critical energy. It may even be possible to translate the Parmenidean thesis affirmed by Zeno – 'The Ent is, the Non-ent is not' – into the eschatological inversions performed (out of Eckhart) by Celan's 'un*entw*orden'.

Plato's *Parmenides* informs us of Zeno's first hypothesis: 'If things are many, then it follows that the same things must be both like and unlike; but that is impossible; for unlike things cannot be like or like things unlike.' Hence 'it is also impossible for there to be many things'.[28] Taken to its extreme, this doctrine abolishes all speculation about being, for no predication which is not identical with its subject is allowed as legitimate. Such logic has the potential to bring inquiry to a standstill; like the arrow of Zeno's seventh paradox, the mind is arrested at every moment of its flight. Celan had engaged a related mode of thought as early as *Gegenlicht* of 1949: '"All things are aflowing": this thought included – and does that not bring everything to a halt?'[29] His paradox exposes proposition to its own performative contradiction. If, from its opening poem, *Fadensonnen* is a text generated by contradiction, that is in part because it proposes, as open to question, a world of analogical relation, of likeness and unlikeness, at its most vexed in the predication of when and where.

The (dis)orientations of these companion poems of place suppose an experience of loss. In each, however, consciousness is directed back to that condition. None tolerates a givenness which, if conceded – as with the negation in '*Un*sterblichkeit' – threatens to become a first term cancelling further inquiry. But what, we might ask, is lost in DIE HOCHWELT?

DIE HOCHWELT – verloren, die Wahnfahrt, die Tagfahrt.	THE WORLD ABOVE – lost, the cantrip, the day trip.

Erfragbar, von hier aus, das mit dem Rose im Brachjahr heimgedeutete Nirgends.	Inquisible, from here on, Nowhere, with the bare-fallow rose taken to mean home. (p. 192)

The participle 'verloren' seems to be shared between the term which precedes it and those which succeed it: 'die Wahnfahrt, die Tagfahrt'. The latter projects a dissonant equivalence between ecstatic transport ('Wahn' may translate delirium) and the more commonly shared pleasure of the day trip, an excursion which presumes a return. Reading within the limits of this first line, each journey (they are conceivably one and the same) has as its only available destination 'the world above'. Yet even if that is so, the absence of a copula not only makes it difficult to determine the loss which is predicated here, but ellipsis further obscures the possible grounds of predication. We may have lost the world above; or, having posited it – as, literally, our point of departure – we may discover it as a place of no return. The 'world above' may presuppose loss; or loss may follow from arrival at this destination.

Such conjecture has, at the same time, to engage with the sense of 'Hochwelt'. Joachim Schulze has suggested that the poem borrows this and its other motifs from an essay by Gershom Scholem on the kabbalistic understanding of the *Shekhinah*.[30] Scholem notes that certain mystical sources distinguish between a feminised higher and lower *Shekhinah* corresponding respectively to the third and last of the *Sefirot*, the ten 'powers' through which an inalienable Godhead is made manifest. Divine emanation in the 'higher mother' of the third of these powers, *Binah* or Understanding, reveals an 'eternal present' to which, in the last instance, all that is creaturely may return. The seven lower *Sefirot* are deemed the children of *Binah*. The last of them, *Malkhut* or Sovereignty, receives the light of the others, and as 'lower mother' participates in and governs the world of creation. The higher *Shekhinah* is represented by images of fullness – of which the best-loved is the rose – and the lower by images of lack, want or absence, among which is 'Brachjahr', the 'fallow year' twinned with the rose in the poem's third line. Schulze suggests that 'Hochwelt' may refer to the realm of *Binah* – the world of emanation – whereas 'Wahnfahrt' and 'Tagfahrt', which remain after that high world is lost, look toward it as agents of its this-worldly principle.

If my own account proves more uncertain before the agrammaticism of the poem's opening line, this hesitation bears especially on the location of the world intended by its opening word. 'Hochwelt' may be held to nominate a World of Emanation, but Celan's deployment of his source material – much of it demonstrably out of Scholem's commentaries – challenges what we make of that inference by refusing the systemic quality of what is otherwise a hermetic lore which affirms a covenantal God and theodicy. Here I share Alfred Hoelzel's demurral before 'those who would make Celan into a kabbalist', preferring to locate Celan in a 'Jewish tradition of challenge and protest brought against God'.[31] The distance between Celan's eschatology and that of his mystical sources, whether Jewish or Christian, can be gauged by its quizzical and provisional reading of the signs of emanation, and specifically the 'Rose im Brachjahr'. The location of this image within DIE HOCHWELT is suspended both by the deictic abstraction of the poem's 'here' (describing a state of loss) and the temporal parenthesis implied by 'fallow year'. The poem's inquiry is directed, 'from here onward', toward the 'heimgedeutete Nirgends' which is, or has been, 'interpreted home' in the company of the 'bare-fallow rose'. The collocation of nowhere and home is, at least here, a question that can be asked, even if the poem calls into question the nature of their alignment. Cautioning against a misconceived utopianism, 'nowhere' returns us to the critical moment that is 'now/here' in that *nirgends* actually signifies the cancellation of *irgends*, or 'elsewhere'. A poem which interprets its subject home might be described as written in a *Geheimsprache*: as Celan's KERMORVAN puts it, 'Wir gehen dir, Heimat, ins Garn'; we step into the 'snare' (ravel or yarn) of homeland.[32] This poem interrogates that operation, not least by placing the neologism *heimdeuten* within the associative field of more familiar compounds such as *heimgehen* (to go home; to die) and *heimsuchen* (to strike home; that is, to haunt or afflict). If Celan's 'heimgedeutete' is permitted to imply *secret* signification, its being quizzed in respect of 'Nirgends' – in the sense of being 'taken to mean home' – consequently removes us from the sphere of the *Geheim* to that of the *Unheimliche* in

Fathomsuns / Fadensonnen

several of its senses.

In his 'Meridian' speech of 1960 Celan asks us to imagine a mode of writing which 'steps beyond the human, projecting itself into an uncanny realm that is turned towards the human' [*in einen dem Menschlichen zugewandten und unheimlichen Bereich*].[33] This formula returns us to the territory of FADENSONNEN, delineating a 'beyond' which challenges our sense of last and first things. Having travelled beyond, we are now turned toward the human, although Celan's prose does not necessarily license a reading of *back* towards (*zurückgewandt*). If the category of the human becomes, like a memory of something yet to come, posthumous in its very conception, this self-haunting follows from its own *Unheimlichkeit* or homelessness. The 'uncanny realm' whose modern analysis was inaugurated by Freud presupposes the unhousing of what is *heimlich* or *geheim*. In Freud's account of 'Das "Unheimliche"', the 'Ich' or 'I' (usually translated by 'ego') is subject to phantasies which it cannot or will not acknowledge; privately held dread or desire assert a life of their own, animating a world which appears to act beyond, if not against, the agency of the 'Ich'.[34] What was once held most singular (and shameful) about being is encountered in a series of doubles which confound the boundaries of self and not-self. This is a state which, as Freud inadvertently demonstrates in his reading of E.T.A. Hoffmann's 'The Sandman', it is fatal to treat as symptomatic of a secret in need of decipherment; for in that case it can only be interpreted home, to the place from which the interpreter deems it to flee. Celan, on the other hand, suggests that 'poetry, like art, moves with the oblivious self into the uncanny and strange [*zu jenem Unheimlichen und Fremden*] to free itself'. In this critical move 'The Meridian' comes to haunt 'The "Uncanny"'.

Celan seeks to locate poetry in that place where one is set free 'as an – estranged – I' [*ein – befremdetes – Ich*].[35] The poem's 'moment' is, it seems, witness to the realising and unbinding of an alienation which itself distinguishes 'the strange from the strange'. Just as an 'I' is at once 'estranged and freed', so, in prospect, the poem is released into 'artlessness', divested of the coat and trousers whereby, in Büchner's *Woyzeck*, 'art comes in the shape of a monkey'. Celan calls Büchner 'the poet of the creature', and 'das Kreatürliche' presents a limit case both for our understanding of 'das Menschliche' and for art's claim to represent that quality. When Celan apologises for 'dwelling' on uncanniness, the verb he uses is *verweilen*; when Faust makes his pact with Mephisto he declares that he will never say to any moment: 'Verweile doch! du bist so schön!' [*Linger! You are so fair!*].[36] According to Celan, the uncanny is 'in the air – the air we have to breathe'; it names the everywhere tangible presence of an immediately past horror. We all must breathe; we breathe in-humanity; but Celan resists the syllogism latent in his own figure of speech. Poetry is, he suggests, capable of an 'Atemwende', a 'turning of breath' which reorientates or reverses a function which is, in the first place, creaturely before it is human. Here is the moment ('Augenblick') which the poem would inhabit. Within this breathing space the poem turns toward 'another' to confirm and set the limit of its own 'radical individuation'. It spends time and hope – 'verweilt oder verhofft' – in the thought of the other, where *verhoffen* (whose accepted sense is 'to scent the air') recalls for Celan what it is to be a creature. For the poem, 'everything and everybody is a figure of this other toward which it is heading'. Both 'Mensch' and 'Kreatur' are sought 'in the u-topian light' [*im Lichte der U-topie*] of an otherness which, however close to a 'naming and speaking I', is never identical with it. Even in the 'here and now of the poem', the other 'gives voice to what is most its own: its time'.

The here and now of DENK DIR, the final poem in *Fadensonnen*, are probably the best documented of any text in the collection, and help to place it at the apex of a complex historical and geographical triangulation:

DENK DIR

Denk dir:
der Moorsoldat von Massada
bringt sich Heimat bei,
   aufs
unauslöschlichste,
wider
allen Dorn im Draht.

Denk dir:
die Augenlosen ohne Gestalt
führen dich frei durchs
   Gewühl, du
erstarkst und
erstarkst.

Denk dir: deine

LOOK YOU

Look you:
the moorsoldier of Masada
commits homeland to heart,
   undying
in the extreme,
against
every barb in the wire.

Look you:
the eyeless without form
lead you free among the
   throng, you
get stronger and
stronger.

Look you: your

eigene Hand	very hand
hat dies wieder	has held this
ins Leben empor-	piece
gelittene	of habitable earth,
Stück	suffered
bewohnbarer Erde	up again
gehalten.	to life.

Denk dir:	Look you:
das kam auf mich zu,	this came to me,
namenwach, handwach,	awake to name, to hand,
für immer,	for all time,
vom Unbestattbaren her.	from the ungraveable. (p. 246)

The poem was begun on 7 June 1967, the day on which Jerusalem's Old City and Temple Wall were regained by Israeli soldiers during the Six Day War; that summer it was published in Switzerland, Israel (in German and in Hebrew translation), and later also in Germany. Reference to 'the moorsoldier of Masada' in the poem's second line establishes an axis between two distinct moments. The first is the last resistance of Jewish patriots against the Roman occupation of Palestine in the mountaintop fortress of Masada in 72–73 CE, a siege which followed the fall of Jerusalem and destruction of the Temple, and which ended in the self-slaughter of Masada's defenders. The second moment concerns the concentration camp established by the National Socialist regime at Börgermoor in Westphalia in the 1930s, remembered for the resistance song of the *Moorsoldaten* interned there.[37] Not only does this song, by its very existence, affirm the central proposition of FADENSONNEN, but its first line can also be read as a cue for the first poem in the later eponymous volume: 'Wohin auch das Auge blicket, / Moor und Heide nur ringsum' [*Wherever the eye travels, / Moor and heath lie round*]. Running through 'Die Moorsoldaten' is the yearning for homeland ('Heimat') which Celan translates into the first paragraph of his poem. Vitally, however, his model refuses any note of lament: 'Doch für uns gibt es kein Klagen. / Ewig kann's nicht Winter sein. / Einmal werden froh wir sagen: / Heimat, du bist wieder mein!' [*And yet we do not mourn. / Winter cannot last forever. / One day we'll declare with joy: / Homeland, you are mine once more!*] In place of *Klage* (complaint, in its familiar and more formal senses, is here a resource either unavailable or exhausted), Celan's poetry – along with 'Die Moorsoldaten' – adopts the adversarial voice of *Anklage*: implicitly or explicitly, it indicts.[38] This attitude of more than mourning bears importantly on the memorial function both described in and performed by DENK DIR, whose title phrase, meaning 'just think' or 'imagine', might also be translated by an admonitory 'remember'. The poem's last paragraph records that 'this came to me, /[…] from the ungraveable' – *this* being either the poem itself or the 'piece / of habitable earth' recovered in its penultimate paragraph. In either case, the provenance of this definite but indeterminate pronoun is the 'Unbestattbare', that which cannot be buried. The traditional function of the memorial event – its laying to rest of the dead – is denied this particular act. There being something implacable about remembrance in DENK DIR, it follows that memory should also prove unplaceable. The poem implicates the refrain of the Börgermoor inmates, which describes a routine of exhumation as much as inhumation: 'Wir sind die Moorsoldaten / und ziehen mit dem Spaten ins Moor' [*We are the moorsoldiers / working spade into peat*].

The memorialising and aspiration towards homeland *becomes* that which cannot be buried, 'undying / in the extreme, / against / every barb in the wire'. In these lines we observe a deformation already discussed in relation to HENDAYE: the 'Stacheldraht' named in the song of 'Die Moorsoldaten' becomes an image whose connotation of sacrifice and atonement is no more acceptable than that of confinement. Remembrance of 'Heimat' becomes in turn a locus of admonition and apostrophe; although, together with the moorsoldier, it is made an intern, 'ungraveable' memory resists interment. Internalised, and against the grain of a past which would otherwise bury it, the 'Unbestattbare' will not be laid to rest. For Jerry Glenn, this significantly anonymous personification 'refers to the millions of victims who can never have a proper burial'; for John Felstiner it fuses 'two halves of one idea: Jewish victims who *could* not be buried and their spirit that *will* not'.[39] Celan's term refuses the fixity of place implied by *Statt*, a noun related to *stehen* and translated by 'stead'. It is a topos which represents the 'instead' of every dwelling place – a prepositional function performed in German by *statt* or *anstatt*. This terrain is, Celan's ellipses notwithstanding, sufficiently visible in a central paragraph of WER HERRSCHT? (p. 36): 'Kugellampen statt deiner. / Lichtfallen, grenzgöttisch, statt / unsrer Häuser' [*Bulletlamps (globelamps) instead your own. / Light-traps, terminal, instead / our dwellings*]. In a world which is, as this poem reports, usurped by falsehood, an elsewhere positive light is here at odds with itself; it may trap or (to what end?) be trapped, threaten as well as illu-

mine. Spirit of place is in several senses 'terminal', for these numi-
nous traps of light are literally 'bordergod-like'; their guardian
deity is Terminus. 'Instead' marks the conflicted liminality of
what is described, an unhousing which demands that we live –
because and in despite of this – with, or in, what is without. The
same concerns inform Celan's apostrophe to the 'irdisch-unsicht-
bare / Freistatt' [*earthly-invisible / franchise*] of DIE TEUFLISCHEN (p.
96). 'Freistatt' (meaning 'asylum') is another place occupied 'in
stead', offering sanctuary against temporal power, or refuge for
– if not from – one's own condition. In the absence of any other
place which can house liberty or give shelter, this place, in spite
of its potential to prosecute rather than protect, is determined
upon. 'Freistatt' is the near neighbour of *Freistaat* ('free state'), and
elects as a synonym *Heimstatt*. The utopian aspect of this place,
however named, is a matter of exigency; it represents a home-
stead in home's stead.

In 'The Meridian', Celan writes that poems are, among other
things, 'paths from a voice to a listening You, natural paths,
outlines for existence perhaps, for projecting ourselves into the
search for ourselves… A kind of homecoming' [*Eine Art
Heimkehr*]. Any quest for the poet's 'place of origin' is, he
confesses, an impossible one. In its place he seeks a *meridian*, 'the
connective which, like the poem, leads to encounters'.[40] In recog-
nising that the place of homecoming toward which the poet steers
is Nowhere, so we must accept that Celan's verse, far from *geheim*,
is rather the contrary – *unheimlich* for sure, and in that measure
ungeheim.

Notes

1 Michael Hamburger, 'Decoding Celan's Messages', *Jewish Quarterly*
   146 (Summer, 1991), 14–16 (p. 16).
2 Celan's phrase is reported by Michael Hamburger in *Poems of Paul
   Celan* (London: Anvil, 1988), p. 27. For Celan's response to the mixed
   reception of *Fadensonnen*, see John Felstiner, *Paul Celan: Poet, Survivor,
   Jew* (New Haven and London: Yale University Press, 1995), pp. 261–2.
3 Barbara Wiedemann, ed., *Paul Celan/Nelly Sachs Briefwechsel*
   (Frankfurt am Main: Suhrkamp, 1993), p. 105.
4 Paul Celan, *Speech-Grille and Selected Poems*, trans. Joachim
   Neugroschel (New York: Dutton, 1971), p. 223. FADENSONNEN was
   initially published in the sequence *Atemkristall* [*Breathcrystal*], which
   in turn forms the first part of *Atemwende* (1967).
5 Paul Celan, *Speech-Grille and Selected Poems*, p. 198; HAWDALAH was
   first collected in *Die Niemandsrose* [*The No-One's-Rose*] (1963).
6 Judith Ryan, 'Die "Lesbarkeit der Welt" in der Lyrik Paul Celans', in
   Joseph P. Strelka, ed., *Psalm und Hawdalah: Zum Werk Paul Celans*

(Bern: Peter Lang, 1987), pp. 14–21 (p.19).

7 Paul Celan, *Breathturn*, trans. Pierre Joris (Los Angeles: Sun and Moon, 1995), p. 254.

8 See Hartmut Steinecke, '*Lieder... jenseits der Menschen*? Über Möglichkeiten und Grenzen, Celans "Fadensonnen" zu verstehen', *Psalm und Hawdalah*, pp. 192–202 (p. 195).

9 See Dietmar Goltschnigg, 'Das Zitat in Celans Dichtergedichten', *Psalm und Hawdalah*, pp. 50–63 (p. 57).

10 Paul Celan, 'Reply to an Inquiry held by the Librairie Flinker, Paris', in *Prose Writings and Selected Poems*, trans. Walter Billeter and Jerry Glenn (Carlton, Victoria: Paper Castle, 1977), pp. 23–4. Celan's prose is collected in volume three of his *Gesammelte Werke in fünf Bänden* (Frankfurt am Main: Suhrkamp, 1983).

11 Paul Celan, 'Speech on the Occasion of Receiving the Literature Prize of the Free Hanseatic City of Bremen', in *Collected Prose*, trans. Rosmarie Waldrop (Manchester: Carcanet, 1986), pp. 34–5.

12 Paul Celan, *Fadensonnen*: Historisch-kritische Ausgabe, 8.2 (Apparat), ed. Rolf Bücher (Frankfurt am Main: Suhrkamp, 1991), pp. 33–4.

13 Franz Rosenzweig, *The Star of Redemption*, trans. William W. Hallo (London: RKP, 1971), pp. 409–10.

14 Translated by Michael Hamburger, *Poems of Paul Celan*, p. 271; see also Hamburger's analysis on pp. 25–6.

15 Meister Eckhart, 'Tractate XI', in Franz Pfeiffer, ed., *Meister Eckhart*, trans. C. de B. Evans (London: Watkins, 1924), p. 352. Pfeiffer's edition is the second volume of his *Deutsche Mystiker des vierzehnten Jahrhunderts* (Aalen: Scientia, 1962 [1857]). Although many of the texts in Pfeiffer have been either queried or superseded, his importance for us is as Grimm's source for *entwerden* and Lexer's source for *Istikeit*.

16 Meister Eckhart, 'Of Diligence', in James M. Clark and John V. Skinner, *Meister Eckhart: Selected Treatises and Sermons translated from Latin and German* (London: Faber, 1958), p. 98; see *Deutsche Mystiker*, p. 570.

17 See Oliver Davies, *Meister Eckhart: Mystical Theologian* (London: SPCK, 1991), p. 109.

18 Meister Eckhart, 'Sermon XII', in James M. Clark, *Meister Eckhart: An Introduction to the Study of his Works with an Anthology of his Sermons* (London: Nelson, 1957), p. 183; see *Deutsche Mystiker*, p. 180.

19 See Davies, *Meister Eckhart*, p. 155; and Pfeiffer, *Deutsche Mystiker*, p. 579.

20 Paul Celan, 'The Meridian: Speech on the occasion of receiving the Georg Büchner Prize, Darmstadt, 22 October 1960', *Collected Prose*, p. 49.

21 Translated by Michael Hamburger, *Poems of Paul Celan*, p. 175; first collected in *Die Niemandsrose*.

22 Paul Celan, 'Conversational Statements on Poetry', *Prose Writings*, p. 45.

23 Paul Celan, 'Reply to H.M. Enzensberger's Question: "Is a Revolution Inevitable?"', *Prose Writings*, p. 46.

24 See Felstiner, *Paul Celan*, p. 222.

25 Louis Jacobs, *The Jewish Religion: A Companion* (Oxford University Press, 1995), p. 23.

26 Marlies Janz, *Vom Engagement absoluter Poesie: Zur Lyrik und Ästhetik Paul Celans* (Königstein: Athenäum, 1984), p. 185.

27 Gilles Deleuze and Félix Guattari, *Qu'est-ce que la philosophie?* (Paris: Minuit, 1991), pp. 48 and 60.

28 R.E. Allen, *Plato's 'Parmenides': Translation and Analysis* (Oxford: Blackwell, 1983), p. 4.

29 Paul Celan, 'Backlight', *Collected Prose*, p. 14.

30 Joachim Schulze, *Celan und die Mystiker* (Bonn: Bouvier, 1976), pp. 48–49. See Gershom Scholem, 'Zur Entwicklungsgeschichte der kabbalistischen Konzeption der Schechinah', *Eranos-Jahrbuch* 21 (1952), 45–107.

31 Alfred Hoelzel, 'Paul Celan: An Authentic Jewish Voice?', in Amy D. Colin, ed., *Argumentum e Silentio: International Paul Celan Symposium* (Berlin and New York: de Gruyter, 1987), pp. 352–8 (p. 356).

32 Translated by Michael Hamburger, *Poems of Paul Celan*, p. 203; first collected in *Die Niemandsrose*.

33 Paul Celan, 'The Meridian', *Collected Prose*, pp. 42–3; I have slightly revised Waldrop's translation.

34 Sigmund Freud, 'The "Uncanny"', *Standard Edition*, Vol. 17 (London: Hogarth, 1955), pp. 217–52.

35 Paul Celan, 'The Meridian', *Collected Prose*, p. 46; other quotations in this paragraph are from pp. 38–52.

36 See Adrian del Caro, 'Paul Celan's Uncanny Speech', *Philosophy and Literature* 18, 2 (1994), 211–24 (p. 214).

37 See Wolfgang Langhoff, *Die Moorsoldaten*, translated as *Rubber Truncheon* (New York: Dutton, 1935).

38 See James K. Lyon, 'Rilke und Celan', *Argumentum e Silentio*, pp. 199–213 (p. 208).

39 Jerry Glenn, *Paul Celan* (New York: Twayne, 1973), p. 152; and Felstiner, *Paul Celan*, p. 242.

40 Paul Celan, 'The Meridian', *Collected Prose*, pp. 53–4.

Introduction   27

I

AUGENBLICKE, wessen Winke,
keine Helle schläft.
Unentworden, allerorten,
sammle dich,
steh.

INSTANTS whose eyewink
no brightness sleeps.
Increase, in every place,
gather yourself,
stay.

FRANKFURT, SEPTEMBER

Blinde, licht-
bärtige Stellwand.
Ein Maikäfertraum
leuchtet sie aus.

Dahinter, klagegerastert,
tut sich Freuds Stirn auf,

die draußen
hartgeschwiegene Träne
schießt an mit dem Satz:
»Zum letzten-
mal Psycho-
logie.«

Die Simili-
Dohle
frühstückt.

Der Kehlkopfverschlußlaut
singt.

FRANKFURT, SEPTEMBER

Blind, aureole-
bearded hoarding.
A maybeetle dream
illumines it.

Behind, rastered by lament,
Freud's gaping brow,

the lamina-
mute tear
bulletins:
'For the last
time psycho-
logy.'

The mimic
daw
breaks fast.

The glottal stop
sings.

GEZINKT DER ZUFALL, unzerweht die Zeichen,
die Zahl, vervielfacht, ungerecht umblüht,
der Herr ein Flüchtignaher, Regnender, der zuäugt,
wie Lügen sieben-
                    lodern, Messer

                              schmeicheln, Krücken
Meineid schwören, U-
unter
       dieser
            Welt
wühlt schon die neunte,
                        Löwe,
sing du das Menschenlied
von Zahn und Seele, beiden
Härten.

CHANCE IS CHEAT, the signs unscattered,
the number, multiplied, unrightly inflorescent,
the Lord is passing near, He rains, He eyes,
as lies flame
          sevenfold, knives
                    connive, staffs
swear manath, U-
under
      this
          world
mines the Ninth,
          lion,
you must sing man's song
of tooth and soul, each
adamantine.

WER
HERRSCHT?

Farbenbelagert das Leben, zahlenbedrängt.

Die Uhr
stiehlt sich die Zeit beim Kometen,
die Degen
angeln,
der Name
vergoldet die Finten,
das Springkraut, behelmt,
beziffert die Punkte im Stein.

Schmerz, als Wegschneckenschatten.
Ich höre, es wird gar nicht später.
Fad und Falsch, in den Sätteln,
messen auch dieses hier aus.

Kugellampen statt deiner.
Lichtfallen, grenzgöttisch, statt
unsrer Häuser.

Die schwarzdiaphane
Gauklergösch
in unterer
Kulmination.

Der erkämpfte Umlaut im Unwort:
dein Abglanz: der Grabschild
eines der Denkschatten
hier.

WHO
RULES?

Besieged by colours, life, bestead by ciphers.

The dial
steals time from the comet,
the blades
tilt,
the name
gilds their feints,
the helmeted touch-me-not
numbers periods in stone.

Pain, as a limax shadow.
I hear it does not get later.
Saddle-fast, the fade and false
here measure even this.

Bulletlamps instead your own.
Light-traps, terminal, instead
our dwellings.

The black diaphanous
juggler's jack
in abject
zenith.

The trophied umlaut in the unword:
your reflex: graveplate
of an apostrophic shadow
here.

DIE SPUR EINES BISSES im Nirgends.

Auch sie
mußt du bekämpfen,
von hier aus.

THE TRACK OF A BITE, in Nowhere.

This too
you must fight,
from here on.

IN DER EWIGEN TEUFE: die Ziegel-
münder
rasen.

Du brennst ein Gebet ab
vor jedem.

Buchstabentreu, auf dem Notsteg,
stehen Hinauf und Hinunter,
den Mischkrug voll blasigen
Hirns.

IN THE EVERLASTING SHAFT: the coctile
mouths
rave.

You sublime a prayer
before each.

Literal, on the distress ramp,
stand Above and Below,
their crater charged with
blistered brain.

SICHTBAR, bei Hirnstamm und Herzstamm,
unverdunkelt, terrestrisch,
der Mitternachtsschütze, morgens,
jagt den Zwölfgesang durch
das Mark von Verrat und Verwesung.

SIGNAL, by harnstem and hertstem,
occulted not, terrestrial,
the midnight archer hunts
by day the song of twelve through
marrow of treason and attaint.

UMWEG-
KARTEN, phosphorn,
weit hinter Hier von lauter
Ringfingern geschlagen.

Reiseglück, schau:

Das Fahrtgeschoß, zwei
Zoll vorm Ziel,
kippt
in die Aorta.

Das Mitgut, zehn
Zentner
Folie à deux,
erwacht
im Geierschatten,
in der siebzehnten Leber, am Fuß
des stotternden
Informationsmasts.

Davor,
im geschieferten Wasserschild die
drei stehenden Wale
köpfeln.

Ein rechtes Auge
blitzt.

DETOUR-
CHARTS, phosphorate,
struck far behind Here by none
but ringfingers.

Godspeed, regard:

the bullet craft, two
digits less its destination,
pitches
into the aorta.

The cargo, ten
hundredweight of
folie à deux,
wakes
in the vulture's shadow,
in the seventeenth liver, at the foot
of the stammering
transmitter mast.

There,
in the rifted watershield, blow
three standing
whales.

A right eye
ignites.

SACKLEINEN-GUGEL, turmhoch.

Sehschlitze
für das Entsternte
am Ende der Gramfibrille.

Die Wimpernnaht, schräg
zu den Gottesbränden.

In der Mundbucht die Stelle
fürs rudernde
Kaisergetschilp.

Das. Und das Mit-ihm-
Gehn übers rauchblaue,
blanke
Tafelland, du.

SACKCLOTH COWL, uptowered.

Eyeslits
for the unstarred
at the end of the gramfibril.

Lashes stitched askant
the godly fires.

In the bay of the mouth,
berth for the feathering
kaiserchelp.

Yes. And its way-mate
over the smokeblue
empty
tableland, you.

SPASMEN, ich liebe dich, Psalmen,

die Fühlwände tief in der Du-Schlucht
frohlocken, Samenbemalte,

Ewig, verunewigt bist du,
verewigt, Unewig, du,

hei,

in dich, in dich
sing ich die Knochenstabritzung,

Rotrot, weit hinterm Schamhaar
geharft, in den Höhlen,

draußen, rundum
der unendliche Keinerlei-Kanon,

du wirfst mir den neunmal
geschlungenen, triefenden
Grandelkranz zu.

SPASMS, I love you, psalms,

palpate walls deep in the You-cleft
jubilate, O painted with seed,

Ever, you are nevered,
forevered, Notever, you,

hei,

in you, into you
I sing the bonestave rasp,

reddest red, harped far behind
the maidenhair, in every hollow,

without, about
the infinite canon of no kind,

you cast me the nine times
twisted, spittled
deertusk crown.

Deine Augen im Arm,
die
auseinandergebrannten,
dich weiterwiegen, im fliegen-
den Herzschatten, dich.

Wo?

Mach den Ort aus, machs Wort aus.
Lösch. Miß.

Aschen-Helle, Aschen-Elle – ge-
schluckt.

Vermessen, entmessen, verortet, entwortet,

entwo

Ashen-
Schluckauf, deine Augen
im Arm,
immer.

YOUR EYES INARMED,
the
burnt asunder,
cradle you still, in the wing-
ed heartshadow, you.

Where?

Put the word out, put the world out.
Quench. Measure.

Ash-hell, ash-ell – en-
gorged.

Unmeet, unmete, unworded, unworlded,

whereout

ash-en-
vomished, your eyes
inarmed,
always.

HENDAYE

Die orangene Kresse,
steck sie dir hinter die Stirn,
schweig den Dorn heraus aus dem Draht,
mit dem sie schöntut, auch jetzt,
hör ihm zu,
eine Ungeduld lang.

HENDAYE

The orange cress
plant behind your brow,
quiet the barb from the wire
which adorns it, even now,
and this attend,
impatience long.

PAU, NACHTS

Die Unsterblichkeitsziffer, von Heinrich
dem Vierten in
den Schildkrötenadel gewiegt,
höhnt eleatisch
hinter sich her.

PAU, NIGHT

The cipher of immortality, cradled in
the tortoise-athel by Henry
the Fourth,
trails Eleatic insults
in its wake.

PAU, SPÄTER

In deinen Augen-
winkeln, Fremde,
der Albigenserschatten –

nach
dem Waterloo-Plein,
zum verwaisten
Bastschuh, zum
mitverhökerten Amen,
in die ewige
Hauslücke sing ich
dich hin:

daß Baruch, der niemals
Weinende
rund um dich die
kantige,
unverstandene, sehende
Träne zurecht-
schleife.

PAU, LATER

In the corners of your
eye, outland,
the Albigensian shadow –

to
the Waterloo-Plein,
to the orphaned
espadrille, to the
Amen thrown in,
I sing you
through the eternal gap
between houses:

that Baruch, he who never
weeps,
may grind to right the
square-edged,
scopic, uncomprehended
tear around
you.

DER HENGST mit dem blühenden Docht,
levitierend, in Paß-
höhe,
Kometenglanz auf
der Kruppe.

Du, in den mit-
verschworenen Wildbächen Auf-
geschlüsselte, die
hüpfenden Brüste im scharfen
Versspangen-Joch,
stürzt mit mir durch
Bilder, Felsen, Zahlen.

STALLION with the flowering rod,
levitant, as the pass
is high,
a cometflare on its
crupper.

You, in the con-
jurate torrents ana-
grammatic, your
starting breasts in the sharp-
yoked verseclasp,
crash with me through
pictures, mountains, numbers.

DIE UNZE WAHRHEIT tief im Wahn,

an ihr
kommen die Teller der Waage
vorübergerollt,
beide zugleich, im Gespräch,

das kämpfend in Herz-
höhe gestemmte Gesetz,
Sohn, siegt.

THE OUNCE OF TRUTH in deep amaze,

past
it roll the pans
of the balance,
as one, conversing,

its campaign raised
high as the heart, the law,
son, overcomes.

IN DEN GERÄUSCHEN, wie unser Anfang,
in der Schlucht,
wo du mir zufielst,
zieh ich sie wieder auf, die
Spieldose – du
weißt: die unsichtbare,
die
unhörbare.

IN THE SOUNDS, as our beginning,
in the abyss,
where you fell to me,
I wind it up again, the
music box – you
know: the invisible,
the
inaudible.

LYON, LES ARCHERS

Der Eisenstachel, gebäumt,
in der Ziegelsteinnische:
das Neben-Jahrtausend
fremdet sich ein, unbezwingbar,
folgt
deinen fahrenden Augen,

jetzt,
mit herbeigewürfelten Blicken,
weckst du, die neben dir ist,
sie wird schwerer,
schwerer,

auch du, mit allem
Eingefremdeten in dir,
fremdest dich ein,
tiefer,

die Eine
Sehne
spannt ihren Schmerz unter euch,

das verschollene Ziel
strahlt, Bogen.

Lyon, Les Archers

The iron barb, rampant,
in the brick niche:
the sideling millennium
stranges within, indomitable,
follows
your travelling eyes,

now,
with dieshot glances,
you wake her beside you,
she is ever
heavier,

you too, with so much
instranged in you,
strange within,
deeper,

beneath you two
the One
sinew draws its pain,

the once tolled mark
blazons, bow.

DIE KÖPFE, ungeheuer, die Stadt,
die sie baun,
hinterm Glück.

Wenn du noch einmal mein Schmerz wärst, dir treu,
und es käm eine Lippe vorbei, diesseitig, am
Ort, wo ich aus mir herausreich,

ich brächte dich durch
diese Straße
nach vorn.

THE HEADS, immense, the town
they build,
behind all joy.

Were you again my plight, by your troth,
and there came a lip, on this side, at the
place I reach beyond myself,

I should see you down
this road
to the fore.

WO BIN ICH
heut?

Die Gefahren, alle,
mit ihrem Gerät,
bäurisch verhumpelt,

forkenhoch
die Himmelsbrache gehißt,

die Verluste, kalkmäulig – ihr
redlichen Münder, ihr Tafeln! –
in der entwinkelten Stadt,
vor Glimmerdroschken gespannt,

– Goldspur, entgegengestemmte
Goldspur! –,

die Brücken, vom Strom überjauchzt,

die Liebe, droben im Ast,
an Kommend-Entkommendem deutelnd,

das Große Licht,
zum Funken erhoben,
rechts von den Ringen
und allem Gewinn.

WHERE AM I
today?

The fears all
with their engines,
lumpen-rustic,

heaven's fallow hoist
forkhigh,

chalkmouthed losses – you
honest tongues, you tables! –
hitched to glimmer-droshkes
in a town unquoined,

– omen of gold, pretended
omen of gold! –

bridges, overjoyed by the river,

love, in the treetops,
construing the out in outcome,

the great light,
scintillate,
to the right of the rings
and all return.

DIE LÄNGST ENTDECKTEN
flüstern sich Briefworte zu,
flüstern das Wort ohne Blatt, das umspähte,
groß wie dein Taler,

hör auch
mein starkes
Du-
weißt-wie,

das hohe Herbei, die Umarmung
ist mit uns, ohne Ende,
auf der Treppe
zum Hafen,

der Stechschritt erlahmt,
Odessitka.

THE LONG DISCOVERED
whisper letter-words,
whisper the pageless word, circumspied,
big as your dollar,

hear you also
my mighty
you-
know-how,

the high come Hither, the embrace
is with us, without end,
on the stair
to the harbour,

the goosestep grows halt,
Odessitka.

ALL DEINE SIEGEL ERBROCHEN? NIE.

Geh, verzedere auch
sie, die brief-
häutige, elf-
hufige Tücke:

daß die Welle, die honig-
ferne, die milch-
nahe, wenn
der Mut sie zur Klage bewegt,
die Klage zum Mut, wieder,

daß sie nicht auch
den Elektronen-Idioten
spiegle, der Datteln
verarbeitet für
menetekelnde
Affen.

YOUR SEALS ALL BROKEN? NEVER.

Go, cedar also
this breve-
skinned, eleven-
hooved perfidy:

that the wave, honey-
far, milk-
near, moved
by courage to complaint,
complaint to courage, again,

mirrors not
also the electron-
idiot who processes
dates for
menetekeling
apes.

II

SCHLAFBROCKEN, Keile,
ins Nirgends getrieben:
wir bleiben uns gleich,
der herum-
gesteuerte Rundstern
pflichtet uns bei.

DEBRIS OF SLEEP, wedges
driven into Nowhere:
we stay ourselves,
the steered-
round star
avows us.

DIE WAHRHEIT, angeseilt an
die entäußerten Traumrelikte,
kommt als ein Kind
über den Grat.

Die Krücke im Tal,
von Erdklumpen umschwirrt,
von Geröll, von
Augensamen,
blättert im hoch
oben erblühenden Nein – in der
Krone.

TRUTH, roped to
the abandoned dream relics,
comes as a child
over the ridge.

The crook in the valley,
beset by clods,
by scree, by
eyeseed,
sprouts leaves in the
blossoming No on high – in the
crown.

AUS DEN NAHEN
Wasserschächten
mit unerweckten
Händen heraufgeschaufeltes Graugrün:

die Tiefe
gibt ihr Gewächs her, unhörbar,
widerstandslos.

Auch das noch
bergen, ehe
der Steintag die Menschen-
und Tierschwärme leerbläst, ganz wie
die vor die Münder, die Mäuler getretne
Siebenflöte es fordert.

FROM NEARBY
water shafts,
grey-green unearthed
by unroused hands:

the deep
yields its crop, inaudible,
without protest.

To salvage also
this, before day
of stone sounds void
the multitudes of beast and man. Even as,
stepping before each mouth and mow,
the sevenfold pipe commands it.

AUSGESCHLÜPFTE
Chitin-
sonnen.

Die Panzerlurche
nehmen die blauen Gebetmäntel um, die sand-
hörige Möwe
heißt es gut, das lauernde
Brandkraut
geht in sich.

HATCHLING
chitin-
suns.

Plated amphibia don
the blue tallith, the sand-
chattel mew
approves, the hideout
lampwick
turns within.

EWIGKEITEN, über dich
hinweggestorben,
ein Brief berührt
deine noch un-
verletzten Finger,
die erglänzende Stirn
turnt herbei
und bettet sich in
Gerüche, Geräusche.

ETERNITIES, long dead
without you,
a missive meets
your yet un-
wounded fingers,
the shining brow
tilts hither
and makes its bed amid
stench and stir.

DER PUPPIGE STEINBRECH
in der Fliesenfuge
des leer-
gebeteten, treibhaus-
haften Asyls,

ein horniger Blick
schläft sich ins halb-
offene Tor ein,

schlaksig
kommt eine über-
mündige Silbe geschritten,

ein erwachter
Blindenstab weist ihr
den Ort zu hinter
den Schimmelmähnen.

DOLL STONEBREAK
in the crazed paving
of the prayed-
out, forcing-
house asylum,

a corneous eye
sleeps through the half-
open doorway,

hobbledehoy
a post-potestal syll-
able accosts,

an awaked
white cane appoints to
it the place behind
the blanchard manes.

DIE ZWISCHENEIN-
gehagelte Hilfe
wächst,

der Namenbau
setzt aus,

die Gletschermilch karrt
die Vollwüchsigen durch
das schwimmende Ziel
ihrer unbeirrbaren
Brände.

TWIXTEN-
hailed help
grows,

denomination
adjourns,

glacial milk draws
those full-grown through
the shimmering end
of their unswerving
fires.

DER GEGLÜCKTE
Mumiensprung übers
Gebirge.

Das vereinzelte Riesen-
blatt der Paulownia,
das ihn vermerkt.

Ungepflückt die großen
Spielzeug-
welten. Keinerlei Dienst
am Gestirn.

In den Kontrolltürmen hämmern
die hundert silbernen Hufe
das verbotene
Licht frei.

THE CONSUMMATE
mummyleap over
the mountains.

Remarked by the lone
macroleaf
of the paulownia.

The great bauble-
worlds
unplucked. Of no service
to the stars.

In the control towers
one hundred silver hooves
hammer free the forbidden
light.

AUF ÜBERREGNETER FÄHRTE
die kleine Gauklerpredikt der Stille.

Es ist, als könntest du hören,
als liebt ich dich noch.

ON A RAINED OUT TRACK,
the small sham ministry of silence.

It is as if you could hear,
as if I loved you still.

WEISSGERÄUSCHE, gebündelt,
Strahlen-
gänge
über den Tisch
mit der Flaschenpost hin.

(Sie hört sich zu, hört
einem Meer zu, trinkt es
hinzu, entschleiert
die wegschweren
Münder.)

Das Eine Geheimnis
mischt sich für immer ins Wort.
(Wer davon abfällt, rollt
unter den Baum ohne Blatt.)

Alle die
Schattenverschlüsse
an allen den
Schattengelenken,
hörbar-unhörbar,
die sich jetzt melden.

WHITE NOISE, bundled,
beam-
tracks
cross the table
with the bottle-mail.

(Which sounds itself, sounds
an ocean, drinks it
in, unmasks
the gangwealed
mouths.)

The One Arcanum
passes forever into the Word.
(Apostates roll
beneath the tree without leaf.)

Every
shadowclasp
on every
shadowhinge,
in and out of hearing,
all now report.

DIE TEUFLISCHEN
Zungenspäße der Nacht
verholzen in deinem Ohr,

mit den Blicken Rückwärts-
gesträhltes
springt vor,

die vertanen
Brückenzölle, geharft,
durchmeißeln die Kalkschlucht vor uns,

der meerige Lichtsumpf
bellt an uns hoch –
an dir,
irdisch-unsichtbare
Freistatt.

THE NIGHT'S
infernal tongueplay
lignifies in your ear,

attended by glances back-
combed springs
forward,

the spent bridge-tolls,
chidden, chisel through
the limestone gorge before us,

the brackish lightsump
barks up at us –
at you,
earthly-invisible
franchise.

DIE DUNKEL-IMPFLINGE, auf
ihrer unbeirrbaren Kreisbahn
rund um die Wunde,
nadelig,
jenseits von Zahl und Unzahl,
auf Botengang, unermüdlich,

die glasharten
Schleifgeräusche der Schrift,

an beiden Säumen
das aufgeforstete
Hände-Revier (du halber
Schein, alabastern),

in der wintrigen Schonung
spricht eine Kiefer sich frei.

THE DARK INOCULATION cases, on
their steadfast circuit
of the wound,
needlelike,
beyond the numbered and the numberless,
apostolic, untiring,

the glass-hard
grinding of script,

on each margin
the forested
hand-chase (you half-
shine, alabaster),

a pinetree acquits itself
in the winter spinney.

DIE ZWEITE
Nesselnachricht
an den
tuckernden
Schädel:

Weggesackt
der lebendige
Himmel. Unter
der jaulenden
Düse,
mitten im ewigen
Blinkspiel,
beiß dich als Wort in den wissenden,
sternlosen
Halm.

THE SECOND
nettle intelligence
to the
combustious
skull:

The living
firmament im-
merged. Under
the howling
jet,
amid the everlasting
lightshow,
bite as a word upon the witting,
starless
halm.

DAS AUSGESCHACHTETE HERZ,
darin sie Gefühl installieren.

Großheimat Fertig-
teile.

Milchschwester
Schaufel.

THE EXCAVATED HEART,
in which they install feeling.

A greater homeland in ready-
made pieces.

Foster sister
shovel.

DIE FLEISSIGEN
Bodenschätze, häuslich,

die geheizte Synkope,

das nicht zu enträtselnde
Halljahr,

die vollverglasten
Spinnen-Altäre im alles-
überragenden Flachbau,

die Zwischenlaute
(noch immer?),
die Schattenpalaver,

die Ängste, eisgerecht,
flugklar,

der barock ummantelte,
spracheschluckende Duschraum,
semantisch durchleuchtet,

die unbeschriebene Wand
einer Stehzelle:

hier

leb dich
querdurch, ohne Uhr.

Fadensonnen

BUSY
mineral wealth, domestic,

thermal syncope,

insoluble
jubilee,

vitrailed
spider-altars in the all-
paramount block,

the semivowels
(still?),
the shadowparley,

dread, ice-just,
clear to fly,

the baroque-immantled,
tonguesluiced shower-room,
semantically translumined,

the blank wall
of a standing-cell:

here

you must live through-
out, without the time.

DIE KOLLIDIERENDEN Schläfen,
nackt, im Maskenverleih:

hinter der Welt
wirft die ungebetene Hoffnung
die Schlepptrosse aus.

An den meerigen Wundrändern landet
die atmende Zahl.

COLLIDING temples,
naked, in the costume rental:

behind the world
unbidden hope
throws out a rope.

Beached on the tidal wound,
the breathing number.

EINGEHIMMELT in Pest-
laken. Am
entnachteten
Ort.

Die Lidschlagreflexe während
der üppigen
Traumstufe
null.

ENHEAVENED in plague
sheets. At the
unnighted
place.

Rapid eye movement during
maximum dream
activity
nil.

WENN ICH NICHT WEISS, NICHT WEISS,
ohne dich, ohne dich, ohne Du,

kommen sie alle,
die
Freigeköpften, die
zeitlebens hirnlos den Stamm
der Du-losen
besangen:

Aschrej,

ein Wort ohne Sinn,
transtibetanisch,
der Jüdin
Pallas
Athene
in die behelmten
Ovarien gespritzt,

und wenn er,

er,

foetal,

karpatisches Nichtnicht beharft,

dann spitzenklöppelt die
Allemande

das sich übergebende un-
sterbliche
Lied.

WHEN I DON'T KNOW, DON'T KNOW,
without you, without you, without You,

they come one and all,
the
elective beheaded, who
lifelong and skull-less sang
the tribe
of the You-less:

Aschrej,

word without meaning,
transtibetan,
shot in the
helmeted ovaries
of the Jewess
Pallas
Athene,

and when he,

he,

foetal,

plucks the Carpathian Nichtnicht,

the Allemande drills
to

the evacuate im-
mortal
song.

EINGEWOHNT-ENTWOHNT,

einentwohnt,

die gehorsame Finsternis: drei
Blutstunden hinterm
Blickquell,

die Kaltlicht-Ozellen
ummuttert von Blendung,

das dreizehn-
lötige Nichts:
über dich, mit
der Glückshaut,
stülpt sichs

während
der Auffahrt.

INHABITED-UNHABITED,

inunhabited,

the hearsum dark: three
blood-hours after
the well of sight,

the coldlight ocelli
bemothered by blinding,

the thirteen-
loteweight Nothing:
over you, with
the caul,
upends

on
the climb.

RIESIGES,
wegloses, baum-
bewürfeltes
Hand-
gelände,

Quincunx.

Die Äste, nervengesteuert,
machen sich über
die schon
angeröteten Schlagschatten her,
einen Schlangenbiß vor
Rosen-
aufgang.

MASSIVE,
pathless, tree-
diced
tract of
hand,

Quincunx.

Branches, nerveducts,
cast themselves upon
the already
crimsoned shadows,
an adderbite before
the rose-
uprise.

GEWIEHERTE TUMBAGEBETE,

Bluthufe scharren
die Denksträuße zusammen,

die Aschen-Juchhe
blättert die Singstimmen um,
hängt die zerstrahlten Topase
hoch in den Raum,

die gewitterpflichtigen
Leichensäcke
richten sich aus,

im Trauerkondukt
grinst unwiderstehlich
das Königreich
Bemen.

BRAYING TUMBA PRAYERS,

bloody hooves
trammel the wreaths,

an ashen huzza turns
the leaves of the requiem,
hangs on high
irradiate topazes,

the stormtrue
body bags
dress ranks,

in the cortège
grins irresistibly
the kingdom of
Bema.

DIE EWIGKEITEN TINGELN
im abgebeugten Strahl,

ein Gruß steht kopf, zwischen zweien,

der dunkelblütige, sich
mitverschweigende
Muskel
kammert den Namen ein, den er mittrug,

und pflanzt sich fort

durch Knospung.

SMALL-TIME ETERNITIES
in the downcast beam,

a handstand salute, between synapsis,

the melanemic, dumb-
covin
muscle
incamerates its cognomen,

and propagates

through the bud.

MÜLLSCHLUCKER-CHÖRE, silbrig:

Das Frieselfieber
läuft und läuft um das Schachtgrab,

wer

diesen Dezember denkt, dem
feuchtet ein Blick
die redende Stirn.

CHOIRS OF SILVER refuse chutes:

Lichen tropicus
chases round the pit grave,

he

who thinks this December,
an eye shall bathe
his eloquent brow.

III

ENTTEUFELTER NU.
Alle Winde.

Die Gewalten, ernüchtert,
nähn den Lungenstich zu.
Das Blut stürzt in sich zurück.

In Böcklemünd, über die vordere, die
Leichtschrift,
auch über dich,
tieferer Mitbruder Buchstab,
eilt, unendlichkeitsher,
der Hammerglanz hin.

UNDEVILLED NOW.
Every wind.

Dominions, undeceived,
make fast the lung stitch.
A reflux of blood.

In Böcklemünd, over the nearer, the
trace-script,
and over you,
more deeply charactered brother,
speeds on, from infinity,
the hammer glint.

HÜLLEN im Endlichen, dehnbar,
in jeder
wächst eine andre Gestalt fest

Tausend ist
noch nicht einmal Eins.

Jeden Pfeil, den du losschickst,
begleitet das mitgeschossene Ziel
ins unbeirrbar-geheime
Gewühl.

HULLS in finitude, elastic,
in each
takes fast another form

Thousand is
not yet simply One.

The shotten mark
attends each dart you loose
into the resolute-hidling
throng.

DIE LIEBE, zwangsjackenschön,
hält auf das Kranichpaar zu.

Wen, da er durchs Nichts fährt,
holt das Veratmete hier
in eine der Welten herüber?

LOVE, straitjacket lovely,
makes straight for the twain cranes.

Who, travelling through the void,
does the breath-spent here,
to one among the worlds, translate?

DU WARST mein Tod:
dich konnte ich halten,
während mir alles entfiel.

YOU WERE my death:
you I could hold,
when all escaped me.

ZUR RECHTEN – wer? Die Tödin.
Und du, zur Linken, du?

Die Reise-Sicheln am außer-
himmlischen Ort
mimen sich weißgrau
zu Mondschwalben zusammen,
zu Sternmauerseglern,

ich tauche dorthin
und gieß eine Urnevoll
in dich hinunter,
hinein.

TO THE RIGHT – who? She-death.
And you, to the left, you?

Pilgrim sickles at the extra-
celestial place
inform a white-grey
flock of moonswallows,
starswifts,

I dip to that place
and pour down,
into you,
an urn full.

DIE ABGEWRACKTEN TABUS,
und die Grenzgängerei zwischen ihnen,
weltennaß, auf
Bedeutungsjagd, auf
Bedeutungs-
flucht.

BROKEN DOWN TABOOS,
and the border crossings between,
diluvial, in
pursuit of meaning, in
flight from
meaning.

WUTPILGER-STREIFZÜGE durch
meerisches Draußen und Drinnen,
Conquista
im engsten
untern Ge-
herz.
(Niemand entfärbt, was jetzt strömt.)

Das Salz einer hier
untergetauchten
Mit-Träne
müht sich die hellen
Logbüchertürme
aufwärts.

Bald
blinkt es uns an.

PILGRIM RAMPAGES through
briny Without and Within,
conquista
in closest,
base em-
brace.
(None can expunge what now issues.)

The salt of a fellow
tear here
submerged
travails the bright
logbook towers
upward.

Soon
it signs to us.

STILLE, Fergenvettel, fahr mich durch die Schnellen.
Wimpernfeuer, leucht voraus.

SILENCE, ferryhag, steer me through the rapids.
Ciliafire, light the way.

DIE EINE eigen-
sternige
Nacht.

Aschendurchfadmet
stundaus, stundein,
von den Lidschatten zu-
gefallener Augen,

zusammengeschliffen
zu pfeildünnen
Seelen,
verstummt im Gespräch
mit luftalgenbärtigen
krauchenden Köchern.

Eine erfüllte
Leuchtmuschel fährt
durch ein Gewissen.

THE ONE self-
starred
night.

Ashenfathomed,
hour after hour,
by shadowed eyes
under sealed lids,

all ground down
to arrowfine
souls,
stopped in their talk
with reptant quivers
breeding aerial algae.

One satis
lantern-shell
traverses a conscience.

BEI GLÜH- UND MÜHWEIN, nekronym
lang vor der Zeit,
laß ich die Gläserwelt – und nicht nur sie –
Revue passieren

und roll mich in ein steifes Segel, mastenstark,
die Enden tief im Hohlzahn eines Ankers,

und leg mir einen Nabel zu, zwischen den Mitten,
aus unter fetten Sternen
in der gerunzelten Flut,
die sie um-eist,
rotgehurtem
Kork.

OVER GLOW- AND MOW-WINE, necronymous
long before time,
I let the goblet world – and not just it –
pass in review,

I roll in stiff canvas, stout as the mast,
ends at milktooth anchor sunk,

and from cork
whored red
among fat stars
in the ice-bound,
crumpled tide,
I furnish a navel, between each middle.

SCHIEF,
wie uns allen,
sitzt dir die Eine
Hörklappe auf,
frei,

und das Gehörlose an dir,
drüben, beim Schläfenfirn,
blüht sich jetzt aus, mit Narren-
schellen an jedem
Kelchblatt.

ASKEW,
as with us all,
the One ear-
piece bestrides you,
free,

and the unhearing in you,
yonder, on the templefirn,
now sheds its bloom, a fool's
bell on every
sepal.

DIE HERZSCHRIFTGEKRÜMELTE Sichtinsel
mittnachts, bei kleinem
Zündschlüsselschimmer.

Es sind zuviel
zielwütige Kräfte
auch in dieser
scheinbar durchsternten
Hochluft.

Die ersehnte Freimeile
prallt auf uns auf.

THE SIGHTED ISLE'S heartscript moraine
at midnight, by the little light
of the ignition key.

There are too many
powers enthralled of an end
in even this
to all appearance starpierced
ether.

The suspired free mile
hurtles upon us.

UNVERWAHRT.
Schräggeträumt aneinander.

Das Öl rings –
verdickt.

Mit ausgebeulten Gedanken
fuhrwerkt der Schmerz.

Die koppheistergegangene Trauer.

Die Schwermut, aufs neue geduldet,
pendelt sich ein.

UNGUARDED.
Each dreamed athwart.

The encircling oil –
coagulate.

With hammered thoughts
pain sets to work.

Headlong sorrow.

Endured anew, dejection's
metronome.

DAS UNBEDINGTE GELÄUT
hinter all der gemanschten Tristesse.

Hilfsgestänge, gedrungen,
im zeitgeschwärzten Emblem.
Frostfurchen der
Devise entlang.

All das bei halbem
Muttermal-Licht.

THE IMPERATIVE PEAL
behind the mess of tristesse.

Bars-suppliant, punch,
on the timeblacked emblem.
Frost fissures
along the device.

All this in the naevus
half light.

DIE EWIGKEIT altert: in
Cerveteri die
Asphodelen
fragen einander weiß.

Mit mummelnder Kelle,
aus den Totenkesseln,
übern Stein, übern Stein,
löffeln sie Suppen
in alle Betten
und Lager.

ETERNITY grows old: in
Cerveteri the
asphodels
ask themselves white.

With mumbling spoon,
from the death vats,
over the stone, over the stone,
they ladle soup
in every bed
and camp.

SPÄT. Ein schwammiger Fetisch
beißt sich die Zapfen vom Christbaum,

aufgerauht von
Frostsprüchen
hüpft ein Wunsch ihnen nach,

das Fenster fliegt auf, wir sind draußen,

nicht ebenzubringen
der Hubbel Dasein,

ein kopflastige,
tiefenfreudige Wolke
kutschiert uns auch darüber
hin.

LATE. A sponge fetish
gnaws chats from the Christmas tree,

a wish hops after them,
chapped by
frost proverbs,

the window flies open, we are without,

the howe of being
will not be levelled,

down by the head,
a joysate cloud
carries us over that
beside.

DIE SÄMLINGE – causa secunda – pachten
das übergewisse
pupillenhörige
Nichts,
das deine – warum nur? – auch heute
hochzuckende Braue
noch säumt, wenn ich hinseh,
um des darunter
vielleicht noch zu leistenden
Augenschwurs willen.

THE SEEDLINGS – causa secunda – hold in feu
the too certain
pupillary
Nothing,
ever hemming, when I look,
your – but why? – today
as always convulsive brow,
for the sake perhaps
of the as yet unwrought
eye-vow below.

DIE HÜGELZEILEN ENTLANG
die niedlichen Streckfoltern zwischen
Bäumchen und Bäumchen,
geißblattumrankt,

Dum-dum-Horizonte, davor,
vertausendfacht, ja,
dein
Hör-Silber,
Spinett,

Tagnacht voll schwirrender Lungen,

die
entzweigten Erzengel schieben
hier Wache.

ACROSS THE HILLTOPS
quaint racks between
sapling and sapling,
twined with honeysuckle,

dumdum horizons, before which,
yea thousandfold,
your
hark-silver,
spinet,

day and night the churr of lungs,

the
unbranched archangels here
stand watch.

KOMM, wir löffeln
Nervenzellen
– die Entengrütze, multipolar,
der leergeleuchteten Teiche –
aus den
Rauten-
gruben.

Zehn Fasern ziehn
aus den noch erreichbaren Zentren
Halberkennbares nach.

COME, let us spoon
nerve cells
– duckweed, multipolar,
in pools empty with light –
from the
rhomboid
fossae.

Ten strands tow
from centres still within reach
the half-within-ken abaft.

ENTSCHLACKT, entschlackt.

Wenn wir jetzt Messer wären,
blankgezogen wie damals
im Laubengang zu Paris, eine Augenglut lang,

der arktische Stier
käme gesprungen
und bekrönte mit uns seine Hörner
und stieße zu, stieße zu.

EXPURGED, expurged.

If we were now knives,
unsheathed as then, eyegleed-
long, in the Paris arbour,

the arctic Bull
would assail,
crown his horns with us,
and set to, set to.

SEELENBLIND, hinter den Aschen,
im heilig-sinnlosen Wort,
kommt der Entreimte geschritten,
den Hirnmantel leicht um die Schultern,

den Gehörgang beschallt
mit vernetzten Vokalen,
baut er den Sehpurpur ab,
baut ihn auf.

SOULBLIND, behind the ashes,
in the sacred-senseless Word,
the unrimed comes striding,
cortically mantled,

its ear's canal dinned
with reticulate vowels,
to analyse, synthetise
the visual purple.

ANRAINERIN Nacht.
Zwerg- und riesenwüchsig, je
nach dem Schnitt in der Fingerbeere,
nach dem,
was aus ihm tritt.

Überäugig zuweilen,
wenn bikonkav
ein Gedanke hinzugetropft kommt,
nicht von ihr her.

NEIGHBOURESS night.
Dwarf or giant, depending
on the slit in the fingertip,
on what
comes out of it.

Eyes agley whenever
a thought drips
through, biconcave,
not of her expressing.

MÖWENKÜKEN, silbern,
betteln den Altvogel an:
den Rotfleck am Unter-
schnabel, der gelb ist.

Schwarz – eine Kopf-
attrappe führt es dir vor –
wär ein stärkerer Reiz. Auch Blau
ist wirksam, doch nicht
die Reizfarbe machts:
es muß eine
Reizgestalt sein, eine ganze,
komplett
konfiguriert,
ein vorgegebenes Erbe.

. . . .

Freund,
teerübergoßner Sackhüpfer du,
auch hier, auf diesem
Gestade gerätst du
beiden, Zeit und Ewigkeit, in die
falsche
Kehle.

GULLCHICKS, silver,
beg from the parent bird:
from the patch of red
on the lower, yellow, bill.

Black – as a dummy-
head will demonstrate –
is a more powerful stimulus. Blue
works also, but not
through colour-response:
the stimulus must be
one of type, schematic,
wholly
configured,
an inherited given.

. . . .

Friend,
you pitch-paid sack-racer,
here too, on this
shore, you spill down
the gullet of time and eternity
the wrong
way.

IV

IRISCH

Gib mir das Wegrecht
über die Kornstiege zu deinem Schlaf,
das Wegrecht
über den Schlafpfad,
das Recht, daß ich Torf stechen kann
am Herzhang,
morgen.

Irish

Grant me right of way
over the cornstair to your sleep,
right of way
over the path of sleep,
the right to cut turf
on the shelf of the heart,
come morning.

DIE STRICKE, salzwasserklamm:
der weiße
Großknoten – diesmal
geht er nicht auf.

Auf der Schütte Seegras daneben,
im Ankerschatten,
neckt ein Name das
entzwillingte
Rätsel.

THE LINES, saltwater taut:
the great
white knot – this time
it will not loose.

To one side, on the sea-grass hatchway,
in the shadow of the anchor,
a name chafes the
otwin
riddle.

TAU. Und ich lag mit dir, du, im Gemülle,
ein matschiger Mond
bewarf uns mit Antwort,

wir bröckelten auseinander
und bröselten wieder in eins:

der Herr brach das Brot,
das Brot brach den Herrn.

DEW. And I lay with you, you, in the mire,
a greasy moon
pelted us with answers,

we crumpled apart
and crumbled together:

the Lord broke the bread,
the bread broke the Lord.

ÜPPIGE DURCHSAGE
in einer Gruft, wo
wir mit unsern
Gasfahnen flattern,

wir stehn hier
im Geruch
der Heiligkeit, ja.

Brenzlige
Jenseitsschwaden
treten uns dick aus den Poren,

in jeder zweiten
Zahn-
karies erwacht
eine unverwüstliche Hymne.

Den Batzen Zwielicht, den du uns reinwarfst,
komm, schluck ihn mit runter.

PROFUSE ANNOUNCEMENT
in the vault where
we with our
gas-flags flutter,

yea, here we stand
in the odour
of sanctity.

A combust
yonder-damp
vents thick from our pores,

in every second
tooth-
caries wakes
an unreaveable anthem.

You too, come swallow down
the twilight crust you threw to us.

AUSGEROLLT dieser Tag:
der vieltausendjährige Teig
für den späteren
Hunnenfladen,

ein ebensoalter
Kiefer, leicht verschlammt,
gedenkt aller Frühzeit
und bleckt gegen sie und sich selber,

Huf-
schläge des Vorgetiers zum
Hefen-Arioso:
es geht, fladenschön-singbares Wachstum,
immer noch aufwärts,

ein schatten-
loser Geist, ent-
einsamt, ein
unsterblicher,
bibbert
selig.

ROLLED OUT this day:
polychiliad dough
for the huncake
hereafter,

a coeval
mud-scumbled jawbone
recalls the first age
and grins at this and at itself,

hoof-
beats of the master-beast
to the barm-aria:
rising, bannock-fair and songful,
ever higher,

a shadow-
less shade, un-
singled, one
undead,
trembles
blessed.

ÖLIG still
schwimmt dir die Würfel-Eins
zwischen Braue und Braue,
hält hier
inne, lidlos,
schaut mit.

OILY still
the die-spot swims between
your brow and brow,
stops here
sometime, lidless,
and looks too.

IHR MIT DEM
im Dunkelspiegel Geschauten,

du Einer
mit der erblickten
stofflosen Leuchtspiegelfläche zuinnerst:

durchs zehn-
türmige Wüstentor tritt
euer Boten-Selbst vor euch, steht,
einen Dreivokal lang,
in der hohen
Röte,

als wär das Volk in den Fernen
abermals um euch geschart.

YOU MANY WITH
one spied in the dark glass,

you One
with the bodiless
reflex glimpsed innermost:

through the ten-
towered desert gate your
herald-self precedes you, stands,
the space of a triphthong,
in the high
madder,

as if the far-strewn folk
were once more mustered round you.

AUS ENGELSMATERIE, am Tag
der Beseelung, phallisch
vereint im Einen
– Er, der Belebend-Gerechte, schlief dich mir zu,
Schwester –, aufwärts
strömend durch die Kanäle, hinauf
in die Wurzelkrone:
gescheitelt
stemmt sie uns hoch, gleich-ewig,
stehenden Hirns, ein Blitz
näht uns die Schädel zurecht, die Schalen
und alle
noch zu zersamenden Knochen:

vom Osten gestreut, einzubringen im Westen,
                                gleich-ewig –,

wo diese Schrift brennt, nach dem
Dreivierteltod, vor
der herumwälzenden Rest-
seele, die sich
vor Kronenangst krümmt,
von urher.

OUT OF ANGELSTUFF, on the day
of ensouling, phallically
united in the One
– He, lifegiving-righteous, slept you toward me,
sister –, upward
streaming through every channel, mounting
to the root-crown:
which, parted,
sets us on high, coeternal,
cantle erectus, skulls
lightning-seamed, superficies
and all
bones as yet unstrewn:

scattered from the east, to be gathered in the west,
                                        coeternal –,

where this script burns, after
three-quarters death, before
the remnant soul
twisting, torqued
by crown-fear,
from the origin.

DIE FREIGEBLASENE LEUCHTSAAT
in den unter Weltblut
stehenden Furchen.

Eine Hand mit dem Schimmer des Urlichts
wildert jenseits
der farnigen Dämme:

als hungerte noch
irgendein Magen,
als flügelte noch
irgendein zu
befruchtendes Aug.

THE FREEBLOWN LAMPSEED
in furrows under
the world's blood.

A hand limned with ancient light
stalks beyond
the bracky dikes:

as if a stomach
continued to hunger,
as if a yet
impregnant eye
continued to fledge.

KLEIDE DIE WORTHÖHLEN AUS
mit Pantherhäuten,

erweitere sie, fellhin und fellher,
sinnhin und sinnher,

gib ihnen Vorhöfe, Kammern, Klappen
und Wildnisse, parietal,

und lausch ihrem zweiten
und jeweils zweiten und zweiten
Ton.

DRAPE THE WORDCAVES
with panther skins,

extend them, felderal felderol,
insign and out,

give them portals, chambers, antechambers
and wildnesses, parietal,

and every second list
their second ever second
note.

DIE HOCHWELT – verloren, die Wahnfahrt, die Tagfahrt.

Erfragbar, von hier aus,
das mit der Rose im Brachjahr
heimgedeutete Nirgends.

THE WORLD ABOVE – lost, the cantrip, the day trip.

Inquisible, from here on, Nowhere,
with the bare-fallow rose
taken to mean home.

DIE BRABBELNDEN
Waffen-
pässe.

Auf der übersprungenen
                              Stufe
räkeln sich die
                    Sterbereien.

THE BABBLING
weapon-
passes.

On the o'erleapt
                        step
the mortified
                   stretch.

... AUCH KEINERLEI
Friede.

Graunächte, vorbewußt-kühl.
Reizmengen, otterhaft,
auf Bewußtseinsschotter
unterwegs zu
Errinerungsbläschen.

Grau-in-Grau der Substanz.

Ein Halbschmerz, ein zweiter, ohne
Dauerspur, halbwegs
hier. Eine Halblust.
Bewegtes, Besetztes.

Wiederholungszwangs-
Camaïeu.

... NOR ANY KIND OF
peace.

Grey nights, preconscious-cool.
Neurocharges, adderlike,
en route
over the metal of consciousness
to memory blebs.

Grey-within-grey of matter.

A half of pain, another, no
lasting trace, halfway
here. A half of joy.
Kinesis, cathexis.

Repetition-compulsion
cameo.

NAH, IM AORTENBOGEN,
im Hellblut:
das Hellwort.

Mutter Rahel
weint nicht mehr.
Rübergetragen
alles Geweinte.

Still, in den Kranzarterien,
unumschnürt:
Ziw, jenes Licht.

NEAR, IN THE ARCH OF THE AORTA,
in radiant blood:
the radiant word.

Mother Rachel
weeps no more.
Borne across,
all that is wept.

Still, in the coronal arteries,
unbinded:
Ziw, that light.

WIRF DAS SONNENJAHR, an dem du hängst,
über den Herzbord
und rudere zu, hungre dich fort, kopulierend:

zwei Keimzellen, zwei Metazoen,
das wart ihr,

das Unbelebte, die Heimat,
fordert jetzt Rückkehr –:

später, wer weiß,
kommt eins von euch zwein
gewandelt wieder herauf,
ein Pantoffeltierchen,
bewimpert,
im Wappen.

THE SOLAR YEAR, to which you cleave,
throw overboard the heart
and heave away, hunger on, coupling:

two germcells, two metazoa,
that was you,

homeland, abiotic,
now demands return –:

later, who knows,
one of you will re-
appear, transformed,
a parmecium,
ciliate,
on the escutcheon.

WEIL DU DEN NOTSCHERBEN FANDST
in der Wüstung,
ruhn die Schattenjahrhunderte neben dir aus
und hören dich denken:

Vielleicht ist es wahr,
daß hier der Friede zwei Völker besprach,
aus Tongefäßen.

BECAUSE YOU FOUND THE SHARD OF NEED
in that waste place,
the umber centuries rest at your side
and hear you think:

Perhaps it's true
that peace bespake two peoples here,
through earthen vessels.

ES IST GEKOMMEN DIE ZEIT:

Die Hirnsichel, blank,
lungert am Himmel,
umstrolcht von Gallengestirn,

die Antimagneten, die Herrscher,
tönen.

THE TIME IS COME:

The brainsickle, bright,
hangs in the sky,
perambulated by gallstars,

the antimagnets, the masters,
sound.

LIPPEN, SCHWELLGEWEBE der Du-Nacht:

Steilkurvenblicke kommen geklettert,
machen die Kommissur aus,
nähn sich hier fest –:
Zufahrtsverbote, Schwarzmaut.

Es müßte noch Leuchtkäfer geben.

LIPS, ERECTILE TISSUE of the You-night:

prospects mount parabolar,
sight the commissure,
here knit fast –:
no through way, black toll.

There must yet be fireflies.

V

MÄCHTE, GEWALTEN.

Dahinter, im Bambus:
bellende Lepra, symphonisch.

Vincents verschenktes
Ohr
ist am Ziel.

Powers, dominions.

Behind, in the bamboo:
barking leprosy, symphonic.

Vincent's gifted
ear
has arrived.

TAGBEWURF: die
lichtdurchlässige Dorn-
schläfe
grapscht sich noch ein
einziges taufrisches
Dunkel.

An der Herzspitze kommt
eine Muskelfaser
sinnend zu Tode.

DAYCAST: the
passlight thorn-
temple
grabs one more
sullen dewfresh
darkness.

At the apex of the heart
a muscle fibre comes
sensibly by death.

REDEWÄNDE, raumeinwärts –
eingespult in dich selber,
grölst du dich durch bis zur Letztwand.

Die Nebel brennen.

Die Hitze hängt sich in dich.

SPEECHWALLS, inwards space –
spooled into yourself,
you howl through to the last wall.

The nebels burn.

The heat hangs in you.

VERWAIST im Gewittertrog
die vier Ellen Erde,

verschattet des himmlischen
Schreibers Archiv,

vermurt Michael,
verschlickt Gabriel,

vergoren im Steinblitz
die Hebe.

ORPHANED in the stormtrough
the four ells of earth,

eclipsed the archive
of the heavenly scribe,

bemired Michael,
beslecked Gabriel,

fermented in the stoneblitz
the heave offering.

BEIDER entnarbte Leiber,
beider Todesblatt über der Blöße,
beider entwirklichtes Antlitz.

An Land gezogen von
der weißesten Wurzel
des weißesten
Baums.

BOTH THEIR excoriate bodies,
both leaves of death against their nakedness,
both their excreate faces.

Brought to land by
the whitest root
of the whitest
tree.

FORTGEWÄLZTER Inzest-Stein.

Ein Auge, dem Arzt
aus der Niere geschnitten,
liest an Hippokrates Statt
das Meineid-make up.

Sprengungen, Schlafbomben, Goldgas.

Ich schwimme, ich schwimme

OVERWHELMED incest stone.

An eye, cut from
the doctor's kidney,
reads in Hippocrates' stead
the manath-makeup.

Whizbangs, sleepbombs, goldgas.

I'm swimming, I'm swimming

ALS FARBEN, gehäuft,
kommen die Wesen wieder, abends, geräuschvoll,
ein Viertelmonsun
ohne Schlafstatt,
ein Prasselgebet
vor den entbrannten
Lidlosigkeiten.

As COLOURS, accumulate,
the essences return, noiseful, at nightfall,
a quarter monsoon
with no place to sleep,
a tinder prayer
before kindled
lidlesskind.

DIE RAUCHSCHWALBE stand im Zenith, die Pfeil-
schwester,

die Eins der Luft-Uhr
flog dem Stundenzeiger entgegen,
tief hinein ins Geläut,

der Hai
spie den lebenden Inka aus,

es war Landnahme-Zeit
in Menschland,

alles
ging um,
entsiegelt wie wir.

THE CHIMNEYSWALLOW in the zenith, fletch-
sister,

the One of the sky-clock
flew to the hour
and into the chime,

the shark
spewed the living Inca,

it was time to plant
the land of man,

all
revolved,
unsealed as we.

WEISS, weiß, weiß
wie Gittertünche,
reihn die Gesetze sich ein
und marschieren
einwärts.

WHITE, white, white
like gridlime,
the laws form ranks,
and march
inward.

UNBEDECKTE. Ganz und gar
Brüstende du.
Entflochten der Brodem vor dir,
im Angesicht aller.
Keines
Atem wächst nach, Un-
umkleidbare.

Der Steinmützenkönig vorn
stürzt von der Steineselskruppe,
die Hände klamm
vorm tittenbeschrieenen
Antlitz.

UNCOVERED. You bosom-
vanity.
The fumes uncoil before you,
countenanced by all.
No one
breathes thereafter, un-
parelable she.

The stonecap king avaunt
drops from the back of the millstone ass,
hands clapped
to his titbane
face.

DER SCHWEIGESTOSS gegen dich,
die Schweigestöße.

Küstenhaft
lebst du dich fort
in den Umschlaghäfen der Zeit,
in Pistenpaar-Nähe,
wo die kegelköpfige Eis-Crew
die Abstellplätze behimmelt.

THE SILENT STRIKE against you,
silent strikes.

Littoral
you live on
in the transhipment ports of time,
by the double runway
where the coneheaded ice-crew
overvault the hardstands.

HAUT MAL

Unentsühnte,
Schlafsüchtige,
von den Göttern Befleckte:

deine Zunge ist rußig,
dein Harn schwarz,
wassergallig dein Stuhl,

du führst,
wie ich,
unzüchtige Reden,

du setzt einen Fuß vor den andern,
legst eine Hand auf die andre,
schmiegst dich in Ziegenfell,

du beheiligst
mein Glied.

Haut Mal

Inexpiate she,
narcoleptic,
by the gods maculate:

your tongue is soot,
your water black,
your stool is bile,

you mouth,
like me,
obscenities,

you plant one foot in front of the other,
place one hand over the other,
huddle under goathide,

you sanctify
my member.

DAS TAUBENEIGROSSE GEWÄCHS
im Nacken:
ein Denkspiel,
mitrechnerisch-göttlich,
für die Allonge-
Perücke,

ein Ort,
zukunftsenthüllend,
stahlfiberfroh,
zur Erprobung
des ein-
maligen Herzstichs.

GROWTH IN THE NECK, big
as a pigeon's egg:
a conundrum,
mathematical-theological,
for the full-
bottom periwig,

a point,
disclosing futurity,
steelfibre-happy,
ready to try
the once
only heartstitch.

ANGEWINTERTES Windfeld: hier
mußt du leben, körnig, granatapfelgleich,
aufgeharscht von
zu verschweigendem Vorfrost,
den Schriftzug der Finsterung mitten
im goldgelben Schatten – doch nie
warst du nur Vogel und Frucht –
der sternbespieenen
Überschall-Schwinge,
die du
ersangst.

WINTERSET field of wind: here
you must live, granular, garnetlike,
scorched by the
nefandous first frost,
signature of darkling within
the yellowgold shadow – yet never
were you merely fowl and fruit –
of the starspat
ultrasound-wing
you
incanted.

DRAUSSEN. Quittengelb weht
ein Stück Halbabend von
der driftenden Gaffel,

die Schwüre,
graurückig, seefest,
rollen
auf die Galion zu,

eine
Henkers-
schlinge, legt sich die Zahl
um den Hals der noch sicht-
baren Figur.

Die Segel braucht keiner zu streichen,

ich Fahrensmann
geh.

WITHOUT. A quince-yellow shred
of mid-afternoon flies
from the drifting gaff,

the oaths,
grey-backed, trim,
roll
up to the prow,

a
gallow's
cord, the number loops
the neck of the still vis-
ible figurehead.

None need strike the sails,

mariner I
advance.

WER GAB DIE RUNDE AUS?

Es war sichtiges Wetter, wir tranken

und grölten den Aschen-Shanty
auf die große Sonnwend-Havarie.

WHOSE ROUND WAS THIS?

The day was fair, we drank

and quired the ashen-shanty
on the great solstice-wrack.

HEDDERGEMÜT, ich kenn
deine wie Kleinfische wimmelnden
Messer,

härter als ich
lag keiner am Wind,

keinem wie mir
schlug die Hagelbö durch
das seeklar gemesserte
Hirn.

HUGGER-MUGGER, I know
the thrash of your hatchling
knives,

none shouldered the wind
steeper than I,

like none other
the hail drove through
my trim cantled
skull.

KEIN NAME, der nennte:
sein Gleichlaut
knotet uns unters
steifzusingende
Hellzelt.

NO NAME that names:
its unison
binds us beneath the
chantstiff
tent of light.

DENK DIR

Denk dir:
der Moorsoldat von Massada
bringt sich Heimat bei, aufs
unauslöschlichste,
wider
allen Dorn im Draht.

Denk dir:
die Augenlosen ohne Gestalt
führen dich frei durchs Gewühl, du
erstarkst und
erstarkst.

Denk dir: deine
eigene Hand
hat dies wieder
ins Leben empor-
gelittene
Stück
bewohnbarer Erde
gehalten.

Denk dir:
das kam auf mich zu,
namenwach, handwach
für immer,
vom Unbestattbaren her.

LOOK YOU

Look you:
the moorsoldier of Masada
commits homeland to heart, undying
in the extreme,
against
every barb in the wire.

Look you:
the eyeless without form
lead you free among the throng, you
get stronger and
stronger.

Look you: your
very hand
has held this
piece
of habitable earth,
suffered
up again
to life.

Look you:
this came to me,
awake to name, to hand,
for all time,
from the ungraveable.

Benighted

Eingedunkelt

In that Dark Durance:
Paul Celan's *Eingedunkelt*

Eingedunkelt is a sequence of eleven poems which Celan published in the Suhrkamp anthology *Aus aufgegebenen Werken* in 1968. This collection of 'abandoned works' by various Suhrkamp authors placed Celan in the company of, among others, Samuel Beckett, Uwe Johnson, Nelly Sachs and Peter Weiss. According to the volume's editor, Siegfried Unseld, Celan's contribution was composed in the first months of 1966, the author having destroyed most of the poems contemporary with its composition.

It is now known that the report of Celan's destruction of these related poems was in error. *Eingedunkelt* has since been issued as a separate volume containing drafts of the eleven poems in the title sequence together with twenty-four previously unpublished poems dating from the period March to May 1966, all but two of which were annotated 'definitive version' by Celan (Suhrkamp, 1991). The new editors of *Eingedunkelt*, Bertrand Badiou and Jean-Claude Rambach, remark that all thirty-five poems belong to a coherent group of papers designated by Celan for 'the poem after *Fadensonnen*' ('für das Nach-Fadensonnen-Poem'). Among these papers, a title page headed *Eingedunkelt* is dated July 1967. However, another title page and table of contents together suggest that all of the assembled poems were at one point or more conceived as part of a larger sequence to be called either *Narbenwahr* [*Scartrue*], *Notgesang* [*Needsong*], or *Wahngang* [*Path of Madness*]. In the event, the first sequence which Celan issued after *Fadensonnen* was *Eingedunkelt*. The translation which is here presented as *Benighted* comprises this work and four of the poems from its penumbra.

The textual history of *Eingedunkelt* confirms a serialism directed against the singularity of lyric self-expression. For Celan, poetry speaks '*on behalf of the other*, who knows, perhaps of an *altogether other*' ('The Meridian'). The reader is one such 'other' in *Eingedunkelt*. This is a work abandoned *to* its readers, and before

it we too are benighted. The poems which begin and end
Eingedunkelt speak in, of and to the first person plural. Both affirm
a solidarity in adversity of the non-identical first and second
persons singular announced elsewhere in the sequence.
Eingedunkelt asks to be read as literally as possible; it describes an
actual darkness. A moral condition is here realised as material,
recalling the *Animadversions* of Milton: 'let us feare lest the Sunne
for ever hide himselfe, and turne his orient steps from our ingrate-
full Horizon justly condemn'd to be eternally benighted'. Celan's
sequence shares with this passage its apprehension of an escha-
tology in eclipse. In poem eight, what is benighted is the 'power
of the keys' – the ecclesiastical authority conferred by Christ upon
Peter and claimed by his successor Bishops of Rome: 'And I will
give unto thee the keys of the kingdom of heaven: and whatso-
ever thou shalt bind on earth shall be bound in heaven: and
whatsoever thou shalt loose on earth shall be loosed in heaven'
(Matthew 16, 19).

There appears to reign in these poems a temporal theology of
negation which the poetry resists but, in turn, cannot be held to
negate. The dialogical intention of *Eingedunkelt* is not commen-
surate with any ready-made dialectic; this is, after all, a
fragmentary sequence of a fragmentary sequence. Yet by that
very token Celan's mutation of the lyric moment refuses the
lament of a lone subject. The 'grief' ('Gram') announced in poem
eleven is 'insurgent' and collective, qualities which mark a
remove from Celan's immediate precursor in the lyric, Rilke. The
'travellers' or 'Fahrenden' of *Eingedunkelt* make reference to those
in the fifth of Rilke's *Duino Elegies*: 'But who *are* they, tell me, these
travellers, a shade / more fugitive even than ourselves?' These
are the acrobats pictured in Picasso's *Les Saltimbanques*. Rilke's
poem describes a forlorn group wrung by a 'never-contented will'
and serving an art whose now practised ease empties it of signif-
icance. His poem protests the 'wearisome Nowhere' of their act,
and proceeds to imagine a 'place we do not know' where – on the
far side of life, before the 'innumerable soundless dead' – authen-
ticity is recovered in the achieved reciprocity of love. Having
forgotten the kind of practical knowledge ('Können') which is
realised only in striving for it – the knowledge, for example, of
how to love – such travellers have possibly ceased to travel.
Rilke's admiration for their enduring human presence is mixed
with the sense that they are little more than a 'plaything' given to
appease some greater 'sorrow' ('Leid'). The concluding poem of
Eingedunkelt remains intent on this side of life, but has no place

for the resignation or pathos which inflects Rilke's ambivalent identification with the acrobats. The figures of the Fifth Elegy perform on a mat which bears the initial letter of 'Dastehn' – signifying that here is where they stand or remain. Celan translates this term into the *aufstehen* or rising up which informs 'aufständische / Gram'. His poem responds to Rilke's question by travelling beyond its initial gesture of incomprehension. Celan declares an alliance between *us* travellers and a grief which, 'not to be usurped', returns us to our identity *as* travellers.

BEDENKENLOS,
den Vernebelungen zuwider,
glüht sich der hängende Leuchter
nach unten, zu uns

Vielarmiger Brand,
sucht jetzt sein Eisen, hört,
woher, aus Menschenhautnähe,
ein Zischen,

findet,
verliert,

schroff
liest sich, minutenlang,
die schwere,
schimmernde
Weisung.

THOUGHTLESS,
against the smokescreens,
the hanging lantern burns
for us, below

Many-branched fire,
seeks now its iron, hearkens
to where, from neighbouring flesh,
a hissing

comes,
goes,

short
minutes spell out
the glimmering,
grave
directive.

NACH DEM LICHTVERZICHT:
der vom Botengang helle,
hallende Tag.

Der blühselige Botschaft,
schriller und schriller,
findet zum blutenden Ohr.

HAVING RENOUNCED THE LIGHT:
the loud, clear day
of the message.

Seedblessed tidings,
shriller and shriller,
discover the bleeding ear.

DEUTLICH, weithin, das offne
Umklammerungszeichen,

Entlassen die Liebenden,
auch aus der Ulmwurzel-Haft,

Schwarz-
züngiges, reif, am Sterben,
wird abermals laut, Beglänztes
rückt näher.

PLAIN TO SEE, far and wide, the open
sign of enclosure,

Lovers released, from the
elmroot prison even,

Black-
tongue, death-ripe,
grows loud again, Beshone
draws near.

VOM HOCHSEIL herab-
gezwungen, ermißt du,
was zu gewärtigen ist
von soviel Gaben,

Käsig-weißes Gesicht
dessen, der über uns herfällt,

Setz die Leuchtzeiger ein, die Leucht-
ziffern,

Sogleich, nach Menschenart,
mischt sich das Dunkel hinzu,
das du herauserkennst

aus all diesen
unbußfertigen, unbotmäßigen
Spielen.

FORCED DOWN from the high-
wire, you ponder
what yet may be expected
of one so gifted,

The mealy-white face
of our assailant,

Set the luminous hands on the luminous
dial,

When, in the way of men,
darkness infiltrates,
which you distinguish

from all these
unrighteous, unruly
games.

ÜBER DIE KÖPFE
hinweggewuchtet
das Zeichen, traumstark entbrannt
am Ort, den es nannte.

Jetzt:
mit dem Sandblatt winken,
bis der Himmel
raucht.

CATAPULTED
over the heads
the sign, dreambright flames
at the place that it named.

Now:
cigar-leaf semaphore
until the sky
smokes.

WIRFST DU
den beschrifteten
Ankerstein aus?

Mich hält hier nichts,

nicht die Nacht der Lebendigen,
nicht die Nacht der Unbändigen,
nicht die Nacht der Wendigen,

Komm, wälz mit mir den Türstein
vors Unbezwungene Zelt.

Do you exhume
the inscribed
bondstone?

Nothing keeps me here,

not the night of defiance,
not the night of compliance,
not the night of existence,

Come, let us roll the great stone
before the untaken tabernacle.

ANGEFOCHTENER STEIN,
grüngrau, entlassen
ins Enge.

Enthökerte Glutmonde
leuchten
das Kleinstück Welt aus:

das also warst du
auch.

In den Gedächtnislücken
stehn die eigenmächtigen Kerzen
und sprechen Gewalt zu.

DISPUTED STONE,
grey-green, let go
to the narrows.

Glow in the dark moons
light
the little world up:

so you were that
too.

In the gaps of memory
stand autarchic candles
and counsel force.

EINGEDUNKELT
die Schlüsselgewalt.
Der Stoßzahn regiert,
von der Kreidespur her,
gegen die Welt-
sekunde.

BENIGHTED
power of the keys.
The tusk governs,
from the chalk spoor,
against the terrestrial
second.

FÜLL DIE ÖDNIS in die Augensäcke,
den Opferruf, die Salzflut,

komm mit mir zu Atem
und drüber hinaus.

WITH DESOLATION pump the eye,
call to sacrifice, salt tide,

enter with me into breath
and out of it.

EINBRUCH des Ungeschiedenen
in deine Sprache,
Nachtglast,

Sperrzauber, stärker.

Von fremdem, hohem
Flutgang unterwaschen
dieses
Leben.

IRRUPTION of the uncloven
into your speech,
nightlight,

spell-stopt, more.

Eroded by the strange,
high tideway
this
life.

MIT UNS, den
Umhergeworfenen, dennoch
Fahrenden:

der eine
unversehrte,
nicht usurpierbare,
aufständische
Gram.

WITH US, pitched
this way and that, but still
travellers:

the one
unwounded,
not to be usurped,
insurgent
grief.

Four Poems from the Penumbra of Benighted

Vier Gedichte aus dem Umkreis von Eingedunkelt

UM DEIN GESICHT die Tiefen,
die Tiefen blau und grau,
das Singende, Gereifte –
du weiß-und-ungenau.

Der stufenlose Abgrund,
er tut sich selber auf –
Es kommt das Sink-und-sinke,
und erst zuletzt der Lauf.

Die Geierschnäbel brechen
sich von dir selber frei, –
Geräusche ihr, kaukasisch,
im Großen Einerlei.

AROUND YOUR FACE the depths,
the blue depths and the grey,
this singing, this ripeness –
you, white and inchoate.

The vertical abyss
unbidden inhiates –
the endless drop is next,
and only then the chase.

From you, and all you are,
the vulture bills tear free, –
o shrill Caucasian rumour
in the Great Monotony.

DIE ZERSTÖRUNGEN? – Nein, weniger
als das, mehr
als das,

Es sind die Versäumnisse
mit den schwatzenden Ringel-
tauben an ihrem Rand,

Blick und Gehör, ineinandergewachsen,
erklettern die Kanzel
über der weithin in Streifen
zerschnittenen Grafschaft,

Eine Sprache
gebiert sich selbst,
mit jedem aus
den Automaten gespieenen
Gedicht oder dessen
kenntlich-unkenntlichen
Teilen.

ACTS OF DESTRUCTION? – No, less
than that, more
than that,

Acts of omission,
the chattering ring-
doves at their rim,

Sight and hearing, incorporate,
mount the pulpit
above a shire carved
far and wide into strips,

A language
spawns itself
with every poem
or couth-uncouth
part thereof
spewed
from the automats.

SCHREIB DICH NICHT
zwischen die Welten,

komm auf gegen
der Bedeutungen Vielfalt,

vertrau der Tränenspur
und lerne leben.

DON'T YOU WRITE
between the worlds,

rise to
the many meanings,

trust the tearstain
and learn to live.

LINDENBLÄTTRIGE Ohnmacht, der
Hinaufgestürzten
klirrender
Psalm.

Vier Gedichte aus dem Umkreis von Eingedunkelt

LINDENBLOSSOM syncope, up
up and away,
the tintinnabulous
psalm.